BEND THE LAWS OF PROBABILITY
WITH THE POWER OF IMAGING.

WHATEVER YOUR MIND CAN
CONCEIVE AND BELIEVE,
YOU CAN ACHIEVE.

WRITE DOWN WHAT YOU WANT TO
DO WITH YOUR LIFE.

NORMAN VINCENT PEALE, one of
the most widely read inspirational
writers of all time, is the best-selling
author of THE POWER OF POSITIVE
THINKING. In addition to serving as
pastor of New York City's Marble
Collegiate Church, he is a prominent
lecturer, radio host, and editor and
co-publisher of GUIDEPOSTS magazine.

POSITIVE IMAGING

The Powerful Way to Change Your Life

Norman Vincent Peale

FAWCETT CREST · NEW YORK

Scripture quotations in this volume are from the King James Version of the Bible.
Material on Peggy Paul is reprinted courtesy of the Tampa *Tribune*.
Material on Steve Stone is reprinted courtesy of *The Evening Sun*, Baltimore, Maryland.
Several of the stories in this volume originally appeared in *Guideposts* magazine.

This book was formerly published under the title *Dynamic Imaging*.

A SPIRE BOOK

Library of Congress Catalog Card Number: 82-10179

ISBN 8007-8484-7

This edition published by arrangement with Fleming H. Revell Company

Manufactured in the United States of America

SPIRE BOOKS are published by Fleming H. Revell Company,
Old Tappan, N.J. 07675, U.S.A.

Gratefully and affectionately
dedicated to longtime friend
and associate Arthur Gordon,
skilled editor and writer,
with thanks for the helpful
assistance he has given in the
preparation of this book

Contents

1	Imaging—What It Is and How It Works	1
2	How the Imaging Idea Grew	11
3	The Concept That Conquers Problems	22
4	How Imaging Helps to Bolster a Shaky Ego	33
5	How to Manage Money Problems	42
6	Use Imaging to Outwit Worry	54
7	Image Yourself No Longer Lonely	64
8	The Three Biggest Steps on the Road to Success	71
9	Imaging—Key to Health?	86
10	The Word That Undermines Marriage	101
11	The Healing Power of Forgiveness	116
12	Imaging the Tenseness out of Tension	127
13	How to Deepen Your Faith	138
14	Imaging in Everyday Life	150
15	The Imaging Process in Making and Keeping Friends	161
16	The Most Important Image of All	172

A Special Note to the Reader

The pages that follow are written in the first person because to have a single narrator is said to lend clarity and unity to a book. But it is misleading because this book is the product of two minds, one masculine and one feminine. My wife, Ruth, and I have worked together for so long that neither of us can function without the other. This is as much her book as mine. It is a team effort all the way through, and I hope the reader will be conscious of that and bestow credit where it is due.

NORMAN VINCENT PEALE

Your sons and your daughters shall prophesy,
your old men shall dream dreams,
your young men shall see visions.

Joel 2:28

Introduction

Suppose a trusted friend came to you and said, "There's a powerful new-old idea that people are talking about, one I think you should be aware of. It's a concept available to all of us that can shape and change human lives for the better in an astonishing way." What would you say?

You'd say, "Tell me about it!" wouldn't you?

That's what I want to do in this book—tell you about it.

The concept is a form of mental activity called imaging. It consists of vividly picturing, in your conscious mind, a desired goal or objective, and holding that image until it sinks into your unconscious mind, where it releases great, untapped energies. It works best when it is combined with a strong religious faith, backed by prayer and the seemingly illogical technique of giving thanks for benefits before they are received. When the imaging concept is applied steadily and systematically, it solves problems, strengthens personalities, improves health, and greatly enhances the chances for success in any kind of endeavor.

The idea of imaging has been around for a long time, and it has been implicit in all the speaking and writing I have done in the past. But only recently has it begun to emerge clearly and be recognized by scientists and medical authorities as additional proof that mind and body and spirit are one indivisible unit, as the Bible has been telling us all along.

Jesus Christ Himself said, "What things soever ye desire, when ye pray, believe that ye receive them, and ye shall have them" (Mark 11:24). That is the great promise that lies behind the theme of this book. Please keep it in mind as you turn the page and start reading *Positive Imaging*.

1
Imaging—What It Is and How It Works

There is a powerful and mysterious force in human nature that is capable of bringing about dramatic improvement in our lives. It is a kind of mental engineering that works best when supported by a strong religious faith. It's not difficult to practice; anyone can do it. Recently it has caught the attention of doctors, psychologists, and thinkers everywhere, and a new word has been coined to describe it. That word is *imaging*, derived from *imagination*.

Imaging, the forming of mental pictures or images, is based on the principle that there is a deep tendency in human nature to ultimately become precisely like that which we imagine or image ourselves as being. An image formed and held tenaciously in the conscious mind will pass presently, by a process of mental osmosis, into the unconscious mind. And when it is accepted firmly in the unconscious, the individual will strongly tend to have it, for then it has you. So powerful is the imaging effect on thought and performance that a long-held visualization of an objective or goal can become determinative.

Imaging is positive thinking carried one step further. In

imaging, one does not merely think about a hoped-for goal; one "sees" or visualizes it with tremendous intensity, reinforced by prayer. Imaging is a kind of laser beam of the imagination, a shaft of mental energy in which the desired goal or outcome is pictured so vividly by the conscious mind that the unconscious mind accepts it and is activated by it. This releases powerful internal forces that can bring about astonishing changes in the life of the person who is doing the imaging.

To illustrate, right here at the beginning, let me tell you four true stories. As you read them, I think you'll see very clearly the imaging principle at work. Here is the first one:

It's wintertime in Cincinnati a generation ago. A cold wind chills the crowds hurrying along the busy street. A young boy—maybe eleven, maybe twelve—has stopped outside the building that houses the city's newspaper, the powerful and respected Cincinnati *Enquirer*. The youngster is not too warmly dressed; his clothes are obviously hand-me downs. Shivering a bit, he is staring through the big plate-glass window, watching the feverish journalistic activity inside.

One figure in particular has caught his eye: a burly man in shirtsleeves seated at a central desk. A green eyeshade shields his eyes from the glare of a light bulb dangling above his head. An unlighted cigar is clamped between his teeth. His desk bristles with scraps of typescript impaled on spikes. Papers overflow from wire baskets. The black headlines of various editions spill onto the floor around him. Activity. Confusion. Chaos. But power emanates from that desk, and the boy in the street can sense it. He knows that this man is in command.

The man spins around in his swivel chair, twists a sheet of yellowish paper into an ancient typewriter, hammers out a few staccato lines. He rips it out, stares at it, takes a black copy pencil from behind his ear, makes a few lightning-swift corrections. He raises his head, barks an order. A copyboy darts forward, snatches the paper, disappears. The shivering witness in the street watches, transfixed.

A huge policeman saunters past, twirling his nightstick.

Impulsively, the boy turns to him. "Officer, who is that man in there—the one with the eyeshade and the cigar?"

"Him?" The blue giant looks down indulgently. "He's the editor, sonny. The editor of the Cincinnati *Enquirer*, that's who he is."

The policeman moves on. Finally the boy goes down the street, looking just as he did before. But he is not the same as before. He is changed. He's no longer aware of the cold wind or the hurrying crowds around him. Inside his head a scene is forming—not just a vague or casual daydream, but a vision of the future that has all the reality, all the intensity of the present. Intuitively, the boy knows that sooner or later what he is visualizing will come to pass. He is sure of it. The scene in his head is a replica of the scene he has just witnessed behind the plate-glass window, with one all-important change. The occupant of the editor's chair, thirty years hence, is himself. Himself, Roger Ferger, a poor youngster with no connections, no advantages, nothing except an image so powerful that it will bend all the laws of probability until they conform to an even stronger, though hidden law.

He goes home with that image fixed in his head. When he says his prayers that night, he relives his dream and asks for help in achieving it. Night after night he does this, unaware that by imaging himself so intensely in that editorial chair, and by reinforcing that image with prayer, he is touching the kingdom of God within himself and releasing forces more powerful than he knows.

How do I know this story? I know because Roger Ferger related it to me years after that memorable day in his childhood. He told me when he was not merely the editor but also the publisher and the owner of the Cincinnati *Enquirer*.

The Image of Her Future

Now for the second story. Again we go back through the years. We are in one of the poorer sections of an Ohio town. A young girl is bending over a metal washtub. She is one of eight children, the daughter of a miner. She is washing her father's overalls.

As she washes her father's overalls, staring now and then out the grimy window at the bleak, familiar symbols of poverty that surround her, an image comes to her. She has had daydreams about her future before, but this is more than a daydream. Diamond clear in her mind is the picture of a college campus, tranquil green lawns, ivy-covered buildings. Graduation ceremonies are in progress, and she sees herself in cap and gown receiving a parchment scroll. She feels the soaring happiness, the sense of achievement, the pride.

But what kind of impossible dream is this? No member of her family has ever gone to college. Mary Crowe has prayed for the chance to go, it is true, but there is no money for such things. The Great Depression has the country by the throat. There is barely enough food on the Crowe family table. Her strange vision must be just a young girl's wistful fantasy, nothing more. And yet, the image of herself receiving the parchment scroll was so vivid, so real.

Consider, now, what happens next. Mary Crowe receives a summons; her parish priest would like to see her. Puzzled, she goes to the rectory, where the good father opens a desk drawer and takes out an envelope. "Mary," he says, "quite a while ago one of our parishioners gave me some money to be used to educate some deserving young person. I've been watching you, and I've decided you are the one. These funds will make it possible for you to have a four-year scholarship at Saint Mary-of-the-Springs. I know you'll make a wonderful record there."

Again, passionate dream into concrete reality. Burning image into tangible substance. Just coincidence? No, because Mary Crowe told me that—incredibly—when she went to Saint Mary-of-the-Springs and saw the campus for the first time, she recognized it. It was the campus she had seen in the vision that came to her while she was sloshing her father's overalls in the battered tin tub in the Crowe family kitchen.

I can't explain that; Mary Crowe couldn't, either. But she did go to college there. She studied hard and got top grades. As graduation approached, she began to think about a career. She knew of a case in her own run-down neighborhood where a life-insurance policy had stood between a poor family and total disaster. So she decided she would like to become an insurance salesperson.

In those days there were almost no women selling insurance. It just wasn't done. It was a man's world. But Mary Crowe "saw" herself as a successful producer. She visualized buyers whose lives would be protected and helped by the insurance they bought. She fixed all this in her mind with tremendous clarity and vividness. Then she went to look for a job as an agent for one of the largest insurance agencies in the city.

The man in charge of hiring turned her down. Flat. Women on his staff? "Go away," he said to Mary Crowe, "you're wasting your time. And mine."

Mary Crowe went away, but the next day she came back. Again she was refused. Again she came back. Again she was turned down. Day after day this went on. Night after night, on her knees, Mary Crowe prayed for patience and persistence and the strength to follow her dream. She closed her mind to doubt. She would not let it in.

Finally the man in charge of hiring was impressed with her dogged determination. "All right," he said. "We'll take you on. But no salary. No drawing account. Commissions only. So go on out and starve."

Mary Crowe went out and started selling, door to door. People listened, because she made them feel that she was primarily interested in helping *them*—as indeed she was. And she didn't starve. Far from it. She became the number-one salesperson for that company. She became a member of the Million Dollar Round Table—the exclusive group of insurance agents who sell more than a million dollars' worth of insurance in a single year. She became a legend in the insurance business. She became, in other words, just what she had *imaged* herself to be—a stunning success.

Well, you may say, those are interesting stories, but they happened years ago. What about the modern world? What about the present day? Let me tell you about Harry DeCamp.

Imaging Helps Heal Harry DeCamp

Harry was also in the insurance business. Quite successful at it, too. But the day came when that success meant little because he was told that he had cancer of the bladder. Inoperable cancer. When he asked how much time he had to live, the doctors couldn't tell him. They gave him some painkillers and sent him home to die.

Harry had never been a very religious man. As he put it, "I had only a nodding acquaintance with God." He thought about praying, but he didn't know how. "I knew God was there," he said later, "but He was some mystical Being, far away. It didn't seem right to start begging after ignoring Him for so many years."

Then two things happened in rapid succession. Someone sent Harry a get-well card and wrote on it, "With God all things are possible" (Matthew 19:26). Somehow that phrase stuck in Harry's mind. It kept coming back to him. Then he picked up an inspirational magazine and read two stories in it. One was about a seriously injured soldier who recovered from near-fatal wounds by creating mental pictures of himself as a healthy, whole individual. The other story was by a cancer victim who claimed that total believing and total faith were the keys to answered prayer, that Christ meant exactly what He said when He told His followers, *"What things soever ye desire, when ye pray, believe that ye receive them, and ye shall have them"* (Mark 11:24, my italics).

Harry DeCamp was not a churchgoer, though he was a nominal believer. After much thought, he decided to believe with total conviction that God could do anything, and that constant prayer backed by real faith could put him in touch with the enormous healing power of the Almighty. In addition to that, he decided to visualize the healing process taking place in the most dramatic form that his imagination could supply.

He began to image armies of healing white blood cells in his body cascading down from his shoulders, sweeping through his veins, attacking the malignant cells and destroying them. A hundred times a day, two hundred, three hundred, he went through this imaging process. He worked at it constantly, day and night. "The images," he said later, "were just as clear as if they were coming in on our TV screen. I could see an army of white blood cells cascading down from my shoulders into my stomach, swirling around in my bladder, battling their way into my liver, my heart. Regiment after regiment they came, endlessly, the white corpuscles moving relentlessly on the cancer cells, moving in and devouring them! On and on the victorious white army swept, down into my legs and feet and toes, then to the top of my body, mopping up stray cancer cells as they went, until at last the battle was over. Day after day I replayed that battle scene in my mind. It made me feel terrific."

Harry DeCamp also kept on with his chemotherapy, although he was convinced he didn't need it. Six months later, when he went back for a checkup, the malignant mass was gone.

Which was responsible for Harry DeCamp's dramatic recovery—the chemotherapy or his intense imaging effort? Some modern physicians would say both. A noted cancer specialist, Dr. Carl Simonton, in conjunction with Dr. Stephanie Matthews-Simonton, has written a book called *Getting Well Again*, in which he expresses his conviction, based on experience with hundreds of cases, that we all participate, whether consciously or unconsciously, in determining our own health. Dr. Simonton is convinced that imaging is a powerful and effective tool available to victims of cancer or any other illness.

I Discover Imaging

Now I would like to tell you about a personal experience that happened to me many years ago. It was through this experience that I first came upon the powerful concept of imaging. And it happened in an unexpected manner.

Ruth and I had started a magazine called *Guideposts*, a spiritual, motivational publication. Beginning with only seven hundred dollars in working capital, the subscription list had risen to approximately forty thousand, but the financial situation had become difficult, in fact almost hopeless.

At this juncture, a meeting of the directors of the magazine was called as we were in imminent danger of being forced to discontinue the project. Present at this meeting was a wonderful lady named Tessie Durlack, from whom we received a dynamic and creative idea, one that changed the entire course of events. And, I might add, that same idea can change your life, too, as it did ours.

Tessie listened to our glum and dismal appraisal of the situation. We had hoped that she might follow an earlier substantial contribution with another monetary gift. But she quickly said she was going to give something much better than money, namely, a vital idea which in turn would lead to prosperity. "The situation," she said, "is that you lack everything—subscribers, equipment, capital. And why do you lack? Simply because you have been thinking in terms of lack. You have been imaging lack so, therefore, you have accordingly created a condition of lack. What you must do now, at once, is to firmly tell these lack thoughts or images to get out of your minds. You must start imaging prosperity instead."

Some of the directors objected that to mount a frontal attack on an unhealthy or negative thought pattern would not exorcise such thoughts but on the contrary would only serve to drive them more deeply into consciousness. Other directors added their opinion that we do not control our thoughts, but they control us. Seemingly disgusted by these expressions, Tessie snapped, "Don't you remember what the great Plato said?" I hadn't the slightest idea what the great Plato had said, but not wishing to reveal my ignorance I asked brightly, "To which of the many familiar statements of Plato do you refer?"

"To one you never heard of," she declared, and forthwith gave a quotation which she attributed to Plato. As I recall, it went something like this: "'Take charge of your thoughts. You can do what you will with them.' So flush out these lack thoughts and do it now," she said. So then and there, we flushed them out, actually "seeing" them troop out of our minds.

She then explained that those lack ideas or visualizations were hanging around in the expectation that they would return soon to the perch in our minds where they had been hospitably entertained for so long. She declared that the only way they could be kept out permanently was by substituting a more powerful prosperity thought to displace them, an abundance or prosperity mental picture. She then asked how many subscribers were needed to guarantee a continuance of publishing and we agreed that one hundred thousand would do it. "All right," she said, "I want you to look out there mentally and see or visualize one hundred thousand persons as subscribers to *Guideposts*, people who have paid for their subscriptions."

Our visualizing was imperfect, to say the least, but she "saw" them, and so powerful was her imaging that we began to visualize them, too. Then, to our surprise, Tessie declared, "Now that we see them, we have them. Let us pray and thank the Lord that He has given us one hundred thousand subscribers." Rather astonished, we joined her in a prayer in which she asked the Lord for nothing, but instead thanked Him for everything in advance, including our one hundred thousand subscribers. In the course of her prayer she quoted that great Scripture, "What things soever ye desire, when ye pray, believe that ye receive them, and ye shall have them" (Mark 11:24).

She had no sooner said "Amen" than Ruth and I, now tremendously excited, looked to where a stack of unpaid bills had been put in front of our directors, fully expecting they would have disappeared. Apparently we thought the Lord might send down some sweet chariot to whisk them all away. But the Lord, when He wants to change a situation, has a better method. He changes people, and changed people change situations.

And that is precisely what happened in this instance. Our hitherto discouraged directors came alive and began to come up with new ideas at a lively rate. Of course, 90 percent of them were not workable, but 10 percent were valid, and in no time at all the bills began to melt away and subscriptions poured in. Today *Guideposts* has not 100,000 subscribers but 3,600,000, and is read monthly by 12 million persons, making it the fourteenth largest magazine in the United States.

This incident and the demonstration of the projected image as a basic law of mind was one of the highlights of our learning experience. Ruth and I at once became aware of the incredible possibilities in the imaging process. We realized the truth that if a person persistently images failure, life will try its best to develop that picture as fact. But if one images success, it will similarly strongly tend to develop that image as fact. From that time until the present, we have studied the principle of imaging and worked with it, testing it in many demonstrations of actual experience under varied circumstances. We have come to the conclusion that this technique is effective in just about all the important areas of living. It is one of the great principles of creative living and is the theme of this book. It must be kept in mind, however, that imaging is not a magic formula that simply, by some kind of mental trick, brings desired results. In an amazing way, it does open doors to problem solving and to goal achievement. But once those doors are open there must be discipline, determination, patience, and persistence if the problem is to be solved or the dream is to become reality. In this way you will find, as we have, that what you can image you can be.

2
How the Imaging
Idea Grew

Imaging surrounds us every moment of our lives; we're exposed to its power from the moment we're born. If a parent is a doctor or a lawyer or a soldier and wants a child to follow in his footsteps, that parental image or dream is bound to have some effect on the growing child. Not a decisive influence, perhaps, because at first the image is only in the mind of the parent. But an influence, nevertheless.

In my own case, my decision to leave the newspaper field after a year as a reporter and study for the ministry was a reflection of my mother's imaging that some day I would become a preacher, like my father. As intensely as only a mother can, she *imaged* me as a *preacher*. She reinforced that image with fervent prayer, and a minister is what I became.

So the images that other people hold of us do impinge on our lives. But the images that affect us most strongly are the *self*-images that we develop as we move through the years. Sometimes these images are positive and strong; sometimes they're negative and weak. I know that as a

11

youngster in various small midwestern towns, I had some pretty negative self-images, only I didn't call them that. I'm not sure the term "inferiority complex" had been invented yet, but if an inferiority complex means a whole nest of inadequacy feelings, that is what I had.

Where did they come from? I'm not at all sure. My father and mother were both unusually able, strong-minded, outspoken individuals. Maybe somehow I felt that I'd never quite measure up to them, or to their ambitions for me. Or maybe it had something to do with my physique, which was slender and lightweight. I was almost frail compared to my younger brother Bob, who was a rough, tough football player. Perhaps I equated being skinny with being inadequate in other ways. Anyway, it bothered me a great deal, and no matter how hard I tried to gain weight, nothing seemed to help.

Another thing bothered me, as it has bothered the children of clergymen from time immemorial, was the fact that I was a "preacher's kid." Growing up in those small towns, as I did, I resented this label. I had the feeling that people expected me to be a goody-goody, that adults would condemn me if I wasn't and my friends would despise me if I was. So this left me tense and overconcerned about the impression I made on other people.

There was still another thing that may have reinforced my image of myself as an inadequate person. If a guest came to the house or a minister came to call, as was the custom among church families, it was the duty of the children of the family to play the piano or recite a poem or otherwise "perform" for the visitors. This ordeal filled me with absolute horror. Whenever I saw guests arriving, I would try to hide. On one occasion, my Uncle Will removed me from the woodshed, where I had taken refuge, and dragged me to the front parlor where, like an early Christian martyr being thrown to the lions, I was compelled to recite "The boy stood on the burning deck," or as much of it as my state of near paralysis would permit.

The result of all these factors was that when I got to college and had to get up occasionally in class and give answers, I acted like what I was: the possessor of a huge inferiority complex.

This self-image of inadequacy might have gone on indefinitely had it not been for something a professor—Ben Arnesson was his name—said to me during my sophomore year. One day after I had made a miserable showing, he told me to wait after class. Then, when we were alone, he said some things that were tough and true and to the point.

He said that I had a reasonably good mind, but that I was not making adequate use of it by being so hesitant and bashful. "How long are you going to be like this," he demanded, "a scared rabbit afraid of the sound of your own voice? You probably excuse yourself by thinking that you're just naturally shy. Well, you'd better change the way you think about yourself, Peale, and you'd better do it now, before it's too late. If you're not able to do it by yourself, if you need help—well, you're a minister's son. You ought to know where to turn. That's all. You may go now."

To this day I remember the emotions that roared through me as I left that classroom and went out into the sunshine that lay like a golden rug across the quiet campus. I was angry, I was resentful, I was hurt, but most of all I was frightened because I knew that what the professor had said was true. A scared rabbit! How far would I get in life if I kept on seeing myself as a scared rabbit?

Life-Changing Experience

I sat down on the steps of the chapel and prayed the deepest, most desperate prayer of my whole life. "Please help me," I prayed. "Please change me. I know You can do it because I've seen You make drunkards sober and turn thieves into honest men. Please take away these inferiority feelings that are holding me back. Take away this awful shyness and self-consciousness. Let me see myself, not as a scared rabbit, but as someone who can do great things in my life because You are with me, giving me the strength and confidence I need."

I don't know how long I sat there on the chapel steps,

but when I got up something had changed. Of course the inferiority feelings weren't all gone; I still have some of them to this day. But the *image* I had had of myself was changed—and with it the course of my whole life.

As the years went by, I began using imaging techniques whenever I wanted to achieve a certain goal. In my second little church, located in Brooklyn, New York, attendance was low; in fact one day I found the sexton dragging one of the back pews out of the building. When I asked him why, he said he was going to chop it up for firewood. "No one sits in it anyway," he explained.

"Put it back," I told him grimly. "Somebody is going to sit in it!" I visualized that pew full, and all the other pews full, and the church filled to capacity. I held that image in my mind. I worked for it with every ounce of strength I had. I made it part of my innovative thinking. And the day came when the image became a reality.

Now and then my old feelings of being inadequate would come back to haunt me, but usually I was lucky enough to discover an image of success that was stronger than my image of failure. One Memorial Day, I remember there was a mass meeting sponsored by the American Legion. Fifty thousand people crowded into Brooklyn's Prospect Park, where the guest of honor was General Theodore Roosevelt, Jr. I had been invited, I thought, merely to open the meeting with a prayer. But when I got there I found that my name was listed on the program as the main speaker.

A wave of panic swept over me. I had no speech prepared. The thought of standing there before fifty thousand people and disappointing them terrified me. I went to the sponsors of the gathering and told them that I couldn't do it. I wouldn't do it. They would have to find somebody else.

General Roosevelt overheard my lamentations. "Son," he said to me, "stop focusing on failure. You're a minister, aren't you? Here you have a chance to minister to all these grieving mothers. You can tell them how much we love them for the sacrifice they've made. You can tell them how proud this country is of the sons and husbands they lost. So get up there and talk, and I'm going to sit right behind you and visualize you loving these people and helping them and holding them spellbound for the next twenty minutes. I have a picture of this in my mind, and it's so strong that I know it's going to happen!"

So, shamed into it, I tried to do as he said. And his image of my succeeding must have been stronger than mine of failure, because the talk went pretty well. Afterward, I remember, General Roosevelt said to me, "Now, you see, if you think you can, or somebody who believes in you thinks you can, why, then you can!"

Perhaps the idea of the power of positive thinking was conveyed to me right then and there. But behind that idea, and in it, and beyond it was the concept of imaging—holding the *image* of yourself succeeding, visualizing it so vividly that when the desired success comes, it seems to be merely echoing a reality that has already existed in your mind.

I didn't grasp that concept fully then, but I kept on using it. In 1927, when I was called to a big church in Syracuse, New York, I met the same problems I had encountered in Brooklyn. Church debts. Low attendance. The sexton actually kept a tall ladder stretched across some of the empty pews in the balcony because it was the easiest place to store it. "Take it away," I told him. "I see that balcony filled with people, not ladders." And in time, it was.

Imaging was involved in our solution to the church-debt problem, too. The debt was fifty-five thousand dollars. It seems small by present standards, but it was a large sum for those days, and it had been on the books for quite a while. I didn't think we could raise enough money to pay off the whole debt; that seemed too optimistic. But I thought we might raise perhaps twenty thousand dollars. And with this in mind I went to see a member of our congregation, a colorful old gentleman named Harlowe B. Andrews.

Brother Andrews, as we called him, was the wholesale grocer who had the reputation of being the smartest businessman in Syracuse. He had the Midas touch; whenever he put out his hand, money just sprang into it. I figured Brother Andrews would contribute something and might tell me how to get the rest.

Brother Andrews lived all alone in an old-fashioned house in the country. So I drove out and told him we were trying to raise twenty thousand dollars to reduce the debt. I also hopefully asked him how much he might care to contribute.

Brother Andrews looked at me over the half-moon glasses that he wore far down on his nose. "Why," he said, "that's easy. Since you are not going to raise the whole debt I will give nothing. Not a nickel. Not a cent." He studied my face for a minute. Then he said, "But I'll tell you what I will do. I'll pray with you."

That didn't fill me with any burning enthusiasm. It wasn't prayer I was after. It was cold, hard cash. But we got down on our knees, and Brother Andrews spoke very freely to the Lord.

An Unforgettable Prayer

This was his prayer: "Lord, here we are. We have to raise some money. Lord, this young minister means well, but he doesn't know the first thing about business or how to do things in a big way. He has little faith. He doesn't really believe in himself or in his ministry. Now, Lord, if he is only going to try to raise twenty thousand dollars, I won't give him a nickel, but if he will believe he can raise the whole fifty-five thousand dollars, I'll give him the first five thousand. Amen."

As that prayer ended, I was pretty excited. I said to Brother Andrews, "Where are we going to get the rest of it?"

He said, "Where you just got the first five thousand. You prayed for it and you got it. Now let's get down to business. There's a doctor downtown who will tell you that he hasn't any money, but I'm on the finance committee at the bank and I know exactly how much he's got. So we're going to pray that he will give you the next five thousand dollars. We'll not only pray, we'll visualize him doing it. The Bible says that if you have faith even as a grain of mustard seed, nothing is impossible for you. So go downtown and see that doctor and ask for that money and get it!"

I went downtown full of qualms and saw the doctor and asked him for a contribution of five thousand dollars. He looked at me and said, "Why, that's preposterous! That's absurd!" Then he was silent for a while. Finally he said, "Well, I can't explain it, but something comes over me as we're sitting here. I'll give you the five thousand dollars."

I jumped in my car, drove back to Brother Andrews's house, and burst in on him. "He did it! He did it!" I cried.

"Why, sure he did," said Brother Andrews. "Listen, son, I sat here all the time you were driving downtown *not* believing he would do it and I just sent a thought hovering over you all the way down there that he *would* do it, and my thought hit him right between the eyes."

I exclaimed, "You know, I saw it hit him!"

He said, "It penetrated his brain and it changed his thinking. But this should change your thinking, too. Just remember, when you want to achieve something, hold in your mind the picture of yourself achieving it. Paint in all the details. Make it as real as you possibly can. And remember this, too: You're never defeated by anything until you accept in your mind the thought that you are defeated. You are never defeated until you accept the image of defeat."

Brother Andrews, you see, understood the difference between positive and negative imaging. He was telling me that you can image victory, or you can image defeat. You can program yourself one way or the other.

In years gone by, a few people had grasped the concept of imaging and were talking or writing about it, although no one seemed to call it by that name. A French psychologist named Coué advised people to say to themselves constantly, "Every day in every way I'm getting better and better." Some people considered this a silly form of mental gymnastics—lifting yourself by your own bootstraps—nothing more. But there was something to it. I, myself, once heard Coué lecture. To illustrate the power of imagination, he asked the audience to visualize a plank six inches wide and twenty feet long laid across the living-room floor. Anyone could walk it with ease and confidence. Then he asked us to imagine the same plank stretched between two buildings one hundred feet in the air. Imagination—in this case the image of falling—would make walking it almost impossible.

A woman named Dorothea Brande wrote a best-seller called *Wake up and Live*. In it she gave a formula for successful living that she had stumbled upon almost by accident. The formula was this: In whatever you attempt, *act as if it were impossible to fail*. This was just another way of saying *image yourself succeeding*.

When I moved from Syracuse, New York, to the Marble Collegiate Church in New York City, this grand old center of worship, with a history going back to 1628, had fallen upon difficult times. The gloom and fear of the Great Depression of the 1930s were everywhere. Only a handful of worshipers were in the pews. It wasn't easy to create and hold an image of a dynamic church filled to capacity with enthusiastic people. But I knew that was what I had to do.

The night I was installed as minister there was a ceremony of great dignity and solemnity. My parents were there, of course. Later, when we walked out into the rainy night, my mother stopped suddenly, put her hand against one of the great marble buttresses of the church, and began to weep. "This old church is so solid," she said, "so strong. You've got to keep it that way, Norman. Tonight it was filled with people hungry for love, searching for guidance. You've got to give them those things, meet those needs. If you do, your church will always be full."

I was deeply moved, and never forgot those words. I took them then as a reminder of a responsibility, which of course they were. But what my mother also did was implant in me a strong subliminal picture of people seeking something, of people coming to the church to find it. She gave me a vivid picture of a church filled with warmth and joy and vitality. That's what I "saw" with my inner eye and that's what I have tried ever since to bring to reality.

There have been moments of discouragement, of course. But it's odd how, almost always, someone steps forward to renew the image of better results. I remember one night when I gave what I thought was a really terrible sermon. Nobody told me it was bad, but they didn't have to—I knew it was a flop. I slunk out of the church and walked along

Fifth Avenue in a state of total despondency. I didn't even want to go home, because I knew my wife, Ruth, would try to cheer me up and I felt I didn't deserve it.

I Apply for a Job

On lower Fifth Avenue near Twelfth Street was a drugstore run by a man named A.E. Russ, a member of the church and a good friend of mine. The lights were still on, and through the window I could see my friend behind the soda fountain. So I went inside and slumped down on one of the stools, looking as dejected as I felt. When Mr. Russ asked what was bothering me, I told him. "I'm in the wrong profession," I said. "I'll never be a decent preacher. How about a job as soda jerk?"

"Mix me a strawberry soda," said A.E., smiling. "Maybe I'll give you a job."

So, in an effort to lighten my gloom, I went behind the counter, squirted strawberry syrup into a glass as I had seen him do, added ice cream and soda, and handed it to him. He took a sip and made a face. "Better stick to preaching!" he said.

But then he grew serious. "Time to close up," he said. "Why don't you come home with me and talk for a while?"

I went along with him because he was one of those people who project warmth and caring spontaneously, and I needed him. He told me not to worry about one bad sermon, or two, or three, or four. "They'll happen sometimes," he said. "Nothing to get despondent about. Don't focus on that. Focus on people and the needs they have."

There was a photograph of his wife on the table and he nodded toward it. "It was rough when I lost her, but some of the things you've said in church helped me a lot. You've helped in other ways, too, maybe without even knowing it. You've pulled me through some trying times. And that's what it's all about, Norman. Meeting needs. Helping people. So you just keep on trying. Don't worry if a sermon goes sour now and then. Just reach out and help people, and that church will always be full."

So there it was again, the image of a great church actualizing itself. Full of people trying to find a wonderful way of life.

I remember one other time when the imaging process worked in a dramatic fashion. It was a stormy Sunday night in Manhattan. Wind howled around the corners of the skyscrapers, sending sheets of rain mixed with sleet swirling along the streets. I was scheduled to talk, as usual, at the evening service. As Ruth and I drove slowly down to Twenty-ninth from Eighty-fourth Street, I became more and more agitated because I was convinced I would be talking to nothing but empty pews.

"This is awful," I said to Ruth. "Terrible. Nobody in their right mind will come out in this weather." I kept on in this negative fashion for block after block. Finally, Ruth could stand it no longer. She pulled the car over to the curb and parked in the drumming rain. "What's the matter with you?" she demanded. "You're always preaching optimism and positive thinking. Now you're just thinking about yourself and whether or not you'll have a large audience." She pointed at the tall apartment houses around us, gray in the rain, the yellow lights of windows shining dully. "Why don't you think about all the people in those apartment houses? Lonely people, hurting people, people who need the message you have to give them? Why don't you visualize them streaming into the church, filling every pew, bringing their needs and their problems, finding solutions? Let's pray about this right now, right here. Let's ask for the church to be full, not to buttress your pride, but so you have people to help. Let's *see* it full, and give thanks that it will be full!"

Somewhat abashed, I nodded. So we sat and held hands and prayed and imaged, visualized. Then we drove on down to the church and—what do you know—we couldn't find a parking space. "Wouldn't you think," I complained to Ruth, "that the pastor of a church could at least have a parking space?"

We finally found one, walked back two blocks through the rain, and the church was jammed, wall to wall, with people still coming, just the way my mother and A.E. Russ had imaged it so many years earlier—and as we had imaged it, reinforcing our image with prayer.

Can it be argued that the church would have been full anyway that night? Of course it can. But who knows how many people who were hesitant or dubious about going felt a sudden impulse to go? Remember what old Harlowe B. Andrews said of that doctor up in Syracuse: "I saw the idea fly in there and penetrate his head and lodge right there in his mind!"

Let the skeptics have their doubts. I prefer to believe that ideas do have wings!

3
The Concept That
Conquers Problems

In my pocket as I write these words is a card I always carry with me. It came to me many years ago, and I have it retyped occasionally because it gets ragged and worn. On it are five lines, as follows:

> The light of God surrounds me
> The love of God enfolds me
> The power of God protects me
> The presence of God watches over me
> Wherever I am, God is!

Why do I carry this card? Because the image that it evokes of a loving, caring God is the perfect antidote to fear, to worry, to anxiety, to just about every problem under the sun. Whenever I'm troubled, I take that card out and let it remind me that there is an all-powerful Being in the universe who loves me and who is only a prayer away.

This is the greatest concept that the human mind can hold. The more intensely you image it, the happier you are going to be, because you will never feel abandoned or alone. That's what religion is all about, that's what churches are all about, that's what Christ came to teach us—that the love of God is available to us uncertain, groping, unsure human beings, all the time, no matter where we may be.

Sometimes, of course, people refuse to accept this wonderful message of reassurance and hope. I have in my library a book entitled *God Is Able* by a former New York City colleague of mine, Dr. John Ellis Large, who was for some years rector of the Church of the Heavenly Rest on upper Fifth Avenue. Dr. Large is a man of much experience in the healing ministry, and in his book he tells of the case of a man named George. This man's wife, Sarah, was one of Dr. Large's parishioners, although she never came to church or had anything to do with the religious life of the church except when she got into trouble.

One day she came to see him and said, "Dr. Large, I shouldn't take your time. I've been on your church rolls, but I'm what is commonly known as 'dead wood.' But," she said, "I have a real problem. It's my husband. He isn't well. He's irritable, he's irascible, he's full of tension, he's on edge all the time. He's a disappointed, frustrated, unhappy man, and he's developed all sorts of symptoms of poor health. He has gone to the doctor, and the doctor says there isn't anything really wrong with him that wouldn't be straightened out if he got his life in order.

"I've tried to talk to him about it," she continued, "but he just ignores me. It's very difficult. He misses one promotion after another at the office. All the men he started out with in his company have moved ahead faster than he. And this fills him with indignation and resentment. I talked with his boss. He said, 'George is contentious, he is not cooperative, he doesn't play ball, he has no enthusiasm and at times he's full of downright meanness.'"

So Dr. Large suggested to this troubled wife, "Why don't you bring your husband to see me?"

"He would never come," she replied. "He has no use for you or any minister or for the church. I can't even get him to pray with me. He says he is fed up with God. He says he doubts there really is a God."

"Well then," said Dr. Large, "let's give him some treatment at home." And he asked her this unexpected question: "What are your husband's sleeping habits?"

"He tosses most of the night," she said, "wears himself out groaning and moaning, but by about five o'clock in the morning he is deep in sleep. I have to wake him up to get him to the office."

"All right," the rector said, "I'll tell you what to do. At five o'clock every morning you get up and sit by your husband and pray for him. Believe that Jesus Christ is there by your husband's side, actually present with you and with him. Image your husband as a whole man—happy, controlled, organized and well. Hold that thought intensely. Think of your prayers as reaching his unconscious mind. At that time in the morning his conscious mind is not resisting and you can get an idea into his unconscious. Visualize him as kindly, cooperative, happy, creative and enthusiastic."

"Why," she exclaimed, "I never heard anything like that before!"

"Well, it's time you did," he told her. "Now go and do it."

She said afterward that she soon got so she didn't need an alarm clock. She would wake up promptly at 5:00 A.M. and hover over her husband in the company of Christ, projecting these thoughts and prayers into his unconscious. For many weeks nothing seemed to happen, but finally George said to her one day, "You know, it's strange how nice everybody has become—people I used to think were hating me and double-crossing me. What's come over them? They're all so nice. Everything is so different."

Some days later he came to her when he got home from work and said, "What do you know! The boss told me today that he is making me a division manager. I asked him why in the world he would do that. And he said, 'Because of the great change in you. You're happy, you're cooperative, you play ball, you're enthusiastic—you're becoming one of the best men we have.'"

His wife never did tell him how he was reached. But the disorder left him. The power of Jesus Christ is very subtle and very skillful. No wonder the multitudes two thousand years ago sought to touch Him, because the power that came out of Him healed them. And today, twenty centuries later, He is still the greatest healer among all the great healers of the world.

Whenever some deeply troubled person comes to me, I try to plant in his or her mind this image of a loving God who, in the Person of Jesus Christ, is a constant companion. "Picture Jesus sitting there beside you in the pew," I sometimes say to the members of my congregation. "When you leave the church, visualize Him walking out with you, strong, compassionate, protective, understanding. Take Him with you into your home. Take Him with you when you go to work tomorrow. And don't think this is some romantic daydream or pious flight of fancy, because He *is* there. He said He would be with us unto the end of the world, and He meant exactly what He said."

Frightened or unhappy people almost always respond to this message. I remember a night years ago—it was during the Korean War—when a phone call awakened me from a sound sleep. It was from a young woman obviously in great distress. She said her soldier husband was overseas in an area where there was heavy fighting. She was afraid he wouldn't survive and come back to her. Her fears had crowded in on her in the dead of night until they seemed overwhelming. "I called you," she sobbed, "because I go to your church sometimes. I don't know where to turn. I don't know what to do."

When something unexpected like this happens, I always say a quick, silent prayer, asking for guidance in what I'm about to say. This time, as I said my prayer, I thought I heard, through the telephone, sounds made by a small baby. So the dialogue between us went something like this:

"Is that your baby that I hear?"

"Yes."

"Is it a boy or a girl?"

"It's a girl."

"Is your baby frightened?"

"No, I'm the one who's afraid."

"Why isn't your baby frightened?"

"I don't know."

"It's because you're with her, isn't it? You love her. The baby knows it. You're there with her."

"But the baby doesn't know what's going on."

"Perhaps not. But she can feel your arms around her, and that makes her feel safe. And that's what you have to do: become like a little child yourself. You have a loving Father, you know. He's with you right now. Picture His arms around you, protective, strong. Be like that baby of yours. Relax—and trust. Do you think you can do that?"

"Well, I can try," she said, and she did sound calmer.

"And one more thing," I said to her. "Thoughts can influence events in ways that no one fully understands. So instead of sending out these fear thoughts, pray for your husband's safe return, with love and hope and confidence. And strongly image him returning safe and sound. Thank God in advance for keeping him safe and bringing him back to you. See him coming through the door, smiling, happy and home again. Hold that image, day and night. We'll say a prayer together now. Then go back to sleep, picturing yourself cradled in the peace and security of the everlasting arms."

Months later that young couple came up to me at the church and introduced themselves. The young soldier thanked me for helping his wife through that midnight crisis. And the young woman told me that she had never really known or felt the nearness of her Heavenly Father until then.

That young woman's problem was the most basic of all problems—fear that threatened her emotional stability until it was driven out by a concept even more powerful: faith in the goodness and nearness of a loving God. As the old saying puts it:

> Fear knocked at the door.
> Faith answered.
> No one was there.

The Biggest Problems Can Be Solved

You are greater than anything that can happen to you. This is a basic fact about human beings and their problems. In big and terrifying crises, people find within themselves a power and a strength and also a wisdom they had no idea they possessed. Of course we believe that these resources come from God, who created every person and who is resident in human nature as well as in the natural world. We also believe that since the Kingdom of God is within all of us, the solutions to problems are also within us. The assumption makes sense.

A woman named Peggy Paul, in her early forties, faced a problem—a really tough problem. Terminal cancer, they called it. But she won a victory over it, according to her story in the Tampa *Tribune* of March 8, 1981, in an article by Tom Berndt. Since a successful application of imaging is documented in this remarkable article, we will give a brief rundown on her handling of the difficult problem that was hers. We follow the newspaper story closely in relating this woman's experience.

There is a striking similarity with that of Harry DeCamp mentioned in chapter 1, except that the use of imaging by Mr. DeCamp was instinctive and without any previous knowledge that any such technique existed. Also in the case of Mr. DeCamp there was a strong spiritual factor. This is not mentioned in that of Peggy Paul, so we must assume the religious element was not involved in her cure. Nor had Harry DeCamp ever heard at that time of the work of the Doctors Simonton.

Ms. Paul was, and is, so we understand, under the care of distinguished physicians, who employed chemotherapy, but as her condition deteriorated and she became fatalistic in outlook, a small incident, the gift of a tray on which were inscribed the words "Don't Quit," coupled with a statement by a nurse that she did not have to die simply because she was told that she was terminal, stirred up her will to live and her will to fight. It was then that she came upon the self-help techniques suggested in the Simonton book *Getting Well Again*. The Simontons, as we understand their viewpoint, believe that psychological forces such as unhappiness and emotional despair are prominent in the development of cancer and conversely the elimination of these factors is important in the cure of the disease.

The immune system or the immunity power of the body seems to be greatly affected by the mental level of unhappiness and emotional distress. The Simontons apparently hold this view and their effort is to develop a joyous and positive life-style to counteract the deleterious effect of negative emotions. Relaxation and visualization are evidently basic in their method. The patient is encouraged to image the white cells in the immune system of the body along with administered drugs, chemotherapy, and other forms of medical treatment involved in the effort, as destroying the malignant cells.

According to the article, Ms. Paul adopted the routine of relaxation and an untensing procedure, meanwhile imaging the progressive destruction of the unhealthy cells by the healthy and powerful white cells. Instead of Mr. DeCamp's method of imaging an army of white cells doing battle with the unhealthy cancer cells, Peggy Paul has her own technique, but one that has also proved effective. She begins by picturing the drug she is receiving in chemotherapy as having the power to break off cancer cells from any tumor and turn them into highly visible orange food, which is then swallowed up by her white blood cells, which she envisions as being rabbits.

She envisions rabbits for a good reason, says Peggy Paul. Rabbits reproduce freely, so there are always lots of them around. And they are always very hungry so they naturally eat lots of their favorite food, the orange-colored cancer cells.

Since the cancer cells can be anywhere in her body, this patient visualizes her hungry rabbits/white blood cells going through her bloodstream everywhere, seeking out and eating the orange food/cancer cells until no more food can be found.

"I need to make sure that there aren't any cancer cells

coming to rest in my chest or anywhere else. So I have my rabbits/white blood cells going up and down my arms and through my whole body, my brain and everywhere. But when they get to my liver area, they really concentrate," she says.

She is said to have also reorganized her positive goals and life priorities. She visualized the battle for health as being gradually won, meanwhile continuing under regular medical treatment. "Finally," says the article, "twenty-two months after her liver cancer was diagnosed, a fourth liver scan confirmed what Ms. Paul had imaged for so long, the tumor in her liver had indeed shrunk. The scan came back with normal results."

It is significant that this patient, rescued from death, thinks that, in the total process of recovery from a malignant condition, her new understanding and control of problems is an important factor. She is quoted as saying, "Today I can tell you that I think the fact that I had this disastrous disease was fortuitous for me. It made me look at myself, it has given me an opportunity to reassess my life's direction and to make goals I have never thought about making before. It also settled a lot of resentment and anger that I had. I was able to resolve those problems and to feel much more secure about who I am in the universe and where I stand. I'm delighted about that."

Peggy Paul, so we are told, gives to all who show an interest a card on which are printed the words "Whatever your mind can conceive and believe, and your heart desire, you can achieve."

And so imaging gave new life to one who could indeed conceive and believe. This is a powerful process but it doesn't have to be a complicated process. Sometimes a simple mental picture can help you get rid of your troubles. I had a letter the other day from a man who said his life had been plagued by all sorts of worries and fears. Then one evening he heard me on the radio giving a talk on the importance of emptying the mind of doubts and apprehensions and negative thoughts. It happened that at that particular moment he was holding in his hand a glass filled with a popular soft drink, clear and carbonated and cold.

As he listened to my talk he looked at the glass and noticed the bubbles rising from the bottom, one by one, moving up through the liquid, reaching the surface, then breaking and disappearing into nothingness.

He said that the parallel struck him so forcibly that he decided then and there that this was the image he would hold in his mind during the day, and especially at night before falling asleep: the image of his worries and fears, like the bubbles, coming from deep within him, rising to the surface and breaking into nothingness. He added that he had tried this technique and "already it is working wonders."

Not a bad idea! If worries make you sleepless, image them as nothing but insubstantial bubbles, and let trust float them away.

Ruth and I feel that trying to help people solve their difficulties is perhaps the most exciting and rewarding thing we do. Day after day the phones ring and the mail pours into our offices from people with every kind of problem under the sun: health problems, money problems, personality problems. Each call, each letter reveals some negative aspect of life that is holding someone back from happiness. "I have a boss who doesn't like me." Or a wife who nags me. Or a husband who is unfaithful. Or a conscience that troubles me. Or a child who defies me. Or a weight problem. Or a drinking problem. On and on. Everywhere, problems. Everywhere, people struggling to solve them.

Half a century of trying to relieve people in distress has left Ruth and me convinced of three things.

1. *Every human being has an enormous problem-solving potential built into him or her*. It's only when that potential is blocked or weakened by defeatist attitudes or negative emotions that problems seem unsolvable or overwhelming.

2. *Problems are an essential and necessary ingredient of life*. They can actually be good for you, although they may be painful at the time. All worthwhile achievements are the result of problem solving. Problem solvers are strong people *because* they struggle to overcome difficulties or adversities. And the reverse is true: People who never have to face problems get soft, mentally and spiritually, just as

people who never exercise get flabby physically. When I hear some troubled person cry, "Why does God let this happen to me?" I often feel like saying, "Because He knows you'll grow and be strengthened if you grapple with your difficulty; He *made* you that way!"

3. *The basic tools of problem solving are available to anyone.* One of the most effective is this technique of imaging. Anybody can experiment with it. There's nothing very difficult about it. And, as I hope to show in subsequent chapters, it can be applied to just about any problem under the sun.

One cautionary word, though, right here at the start. Make the Lord a silent partner in all forms of imaging, because He is the touchstone that will keep your desires on the high plane of morality where they belong. Imaging can be applied to unworthy goals as well as worthy ones. Praying about goals is essential, because if there are any selfish aims or sinful motives, they will appear as you pray. Pray to be sure your goal is right, for if it isn't right it is wrong, and nothing that is wrong ever turned out right.

A wise man once said, "Be very careful what you wish for, because you may get it." That applies to imaging even more forcefully: if you image something long enough and hard enough, you *will* get it.

I remember a somber story of misused imaging that my psychiatrist friend Dr. Smiley Blanton once told me without mentioning any names. A famous Hollywood producer came to him, Smiley said, because things were going so badly in his life. He said he had lost his grip, his career had fallen apart, he couldn't sleep, he was miserably unhappy, and so on.

Finally the inner story emerged. The producer had met an attractive young actress who was trying to get started in films. It was the old story. Although he was married, he decided to have an affair with her. The girl had scruples and resisted, but the producer was a persuasive and determined man, willing to use the power of his position. Also, he was aware of the power of imaging, and he used it to visualize the whole course of the seduction: buildup, timing, setting—he planned it like one of his scenarios. The outcome was just as he imaged it.

But then the girl came to him and told him that she was pregnant. She thought he loved her, perhaps enough to get a divorce and marry her. Instead, he told her to go and have an abortion. She went back to her apartment and took a fatal dose of sleeping pills, leaving a note that implicated the producer. Even in jaded Hollywood, it was a scandal. The man's career was ruined.

So never fail to hold your imaging goals up to the light before you set about achieving them.

In the remaining sections of this book, which we have worked on together, Ruth and I plan to take some of the most common problems that plague and challenge human beings and show how imaging can be used to help solve them. Before you move on to those sections, here's a simple imaging technique that you may find helpful if some stubborn problem is harassing you or troubling you. Take thirty seconds right now and picture yourself taking command over that problem. See yourself solving it, overcoming it, moving beyond it into a realm of confidence where other problems will be met and mastered as they arise.

Then take three long, deep breaths and exhale slowly after each one.

As you take the first one, say to yourself, "I'm breathing in confidence; I'm breathing out fear."

With the second: "I'm breathing in victory over my problem (name it); I'm breathing out defeat."

Then as you turn the page, visualize new confidence and determination flowing into you. You *can* take control of your problems. You *can* take command of your life. This book about imaging is designed to help you do it—and it will!

4
How Imaging Helps to Bolster a Shaky Ego

Dr. Smiley Blanton, famous psychiatrist and one of the wisest men I've ever known, used to say that day in and day out the most common problem he was called upon to deal with in his patients was lack of self-esteem. Most of the people who consulted him, Smiley said, were deficient in self-love. They had a poor opinion—that is to say, a poor image—of themselves. And this great doctor, who knew the Bible backward and forward, always referred such people to the second great commandment: "Thou shalt love thy neighbor *as thyself*" (Matthew 22:39, my italics).

"There it is," Dr. Smiley Blanton would say. "Plain as the nose on your face. Love is the answer to all human ills. But the Bible says here"—and he would thrust the Book right into the patient's hands—"that you can't love anyone properly as long as you despise or downgrade yourself. Look! There it is, right there. See? Right there!"

Inferiority complex: how would you define it? I think I'd say it was timidity in the presence of life. And Smiley was right: it is very common. I have found in my own counseling experience that often the most outwardly confident and aggressive people are using that apparent confidence as a mask for deep doubts about themselves and their ability to cope with the challenges and problems of living.

It's a paradox, really. God made a masterpiece when He created human beings. The Bible says we rank just a little lower than the angels, which is pretty high on the scale of things. It says He crowned us with glory and honor. Now you'd think that a creature made in God's image would be pretty sure of himself, wouldn't you? But all too often he's not. Something holds him back from the belief in himself that makes for happiness. And—as anyone who suffers from a sense of inferiority will tell you—when a person's inner image of himself drops below a certain level, the result is pure misery.

It's almost as if there were two separate, warring entities inside each of us: the strong and the weak, the bold and the fearful, the large and the small. Each of us has a "big me" and a "little me" inside, and many times the "little me" frustrates and paralyzes the "big me."

I remember reading some years ago about the famous Italian tenor Enrico Caruso, surely one of the greatest masters of song ever to step onto a stage. In later life, his confidence was enormous, but at the beginning of his career he was unsure and uncertain.

One opening night at the opera, Caruso was standing in the wings waiting to go on when he was seized by an overwhelming attack of stage fright. His throat became constricted. Perspiration poured from him. He was actually shaking with fear.

Then the stagehands nearby were astonished to hear him say, in a whispered command, "Out! You miserable 'little me,' get out of my way! Out! Out!"

By a tremendous effort of will, Caruso was changing his self-image. He was saying to the fearful, timid element inside of him that the strong, positive element inside him must prevail, would prevail, and in the face of this fierce counterattack, the "little me" shrank away. He went onstage, where he sang with the beauty and power that were characteristic of the great Caruso. At the end, the audience surged up, shouting "Bravo!" Were they applauding the skill of a great artist? Yes, but perhaps intuitively they were acclaiming something more—the man who brought the "big me" out of himself by overcoming the fears and frustrations of the "little me."

I told that story one time to a young wife who came to consult me. She was upset and frightened. Her husband was under consideration for a promotion, and important one. But it was the custom of that particular company to have a party at which top executives had a chance to observe the employee under social conditions. Wives were always asked to this affair, because the company believed, quite rightly, that a man and his wife are an inseparable team—when you deal with one you are dealing with the other.

I said to this young woman, "Why are you so concerned? You are able to handle yourself."

"Oh, Dr. Peale," she said, and her eyes were actually full of tears, "all those other wives have been to colleges like Smith or Vassar or Wellesley. I never got past high school. They'll talk about things I'm not familiar with. I just know I'll be so tense I'll say or do something dumb and ruin Jim's chances for this promotion. I can't bring myself to go, and yet I can't refuse to go. Oh, what shall I do?"

Timidity, you see, timidity even in the presence of a routine situation.

I said to her, "Look, you're a very pretty girl; you dress well; you have honesty and your own quiet charm. Don't worry about those wives from Wellesley. They don't know all that much, anyway. Just be yourself. The trouble with a lot of people is that they always try to copy somebody else. If the Creator wanted us all to be alike, He would have made us that way. You are the only person in the world like you. Think of that: millions of people and only one like you! You are unique and very special. So you just walk into that party and be yourself, your own attractive self. Mix right in with those people and you will shake off this inferiority complex. Go among them saying to yourself, 'I can do all things through Christ who strengthens me.' Just image yourself as charming, natural, and likable and you will come off okay."

Then I told her the Caruso story, and finally she went away a little less frightened, a little less tense, a little more hopeful, and later I heard that the party went very well. Her husband got the promotion.

But there are millions of people who don't know how to shake off doubts and fears, millions who crawl through life on their hands and knees instead of standing tall and proud. I sympathize with them from the bottom of my heart, because I know what psychic pain is like.

Bolstering Your Ego

So what can you do if you have an ego that needs bolstering? How can you stop imaging yourself as an inadequate person—an attitude that just perpetuates the state of affairs you want to avoid?

The first thing is, examine your entire life and see if you can pinpoint some specific cause for these inferiority feelings. Often the cause goes back to childhood. Certainly we're not born with inferiority feelings; a healthy baby has a strong ego and—so far as one can tell—a high opinion of himself. But even so, that self-confidence can be damaged, sometimes by a harsh or hypercritical parent, sometimes by other children who tease or ridicule, sometimes by siblings who outshine or overshadow a sensitive brother or sister.

I remember one man who came to the Institutes of Religion and Health, a counseling service founded by Dr. Blanton and me some thirty years ago. He was seeking help because he felt so wretchedly inadequate most of the time. He just felt that he couldn't cope. And believe me, the "I can't cope" feeling is widespread. Finally, after long discussion and probing, it was found that as a small boy he had nearly drowned in a swimming pool. His frantic mother forbade him ever to go in the water again. He would stand by the pool watching the other boys swim, and gradually the idea took hold of him that he couldn't do what the others did. Thus his disbelief in himself began to grow.

He grew up filled with fear, and when we saw him his talk was full of symbolic references. "This is over my head," he would say. Or, "This is too deep for me." Or, "If I try that, I'll be sunk." This man struggled so hard against a constant conviction of inadequacy that he was close to a nervous breakdown. I told him, as I tell everyone who has an inferiority complex, that the basic answer to the problem is to get a deep sense of the presence of God in your life. Image yourself walking alongside the Power that created the tiniest flower and holds the constellations in their places. This is the surest way to cast out all fear and shrinking and sense of failure. No matter how fearful you think you are, I will guarantee that if you get your consciousness filled to overflowing with God, you will not be afraid of anything in this world. You will walk through life erect, head held high, unafraid.

How do you do it? Well, the answers have been given so often that they sound hackneyed and trite, but they are eternally true. You pray—which is conversation with God. You go where God is talked about and thought about and focused on—and that is usually in church or some good spiritual group, of which there are many. You read the Bible and apply what you read to yourself. There is no great benefit in reading the Bible just because somebody says you ought to. The Bible only comes to your rescue when you take its message and diligently apply it to yourself and your problems and to the image you have of yourself.

Take the story of David and Goliath, for instance. Everyone knows how the slender shepherd boy went out against the great armored giant of the Philistines. Where were his weapons? A sling and five smooth stones, you say? True enough, but that was only *part* of his armament, indeed the smallest part. Listen to the words of David himself as he went out to face what everyone else thought was certain death. "Thou [Goliath] comest to me with a sword, and with a spear, and with a shield: but I come to thee in the name of the Lord of hosts..." (1 Samuel 17:45).

In other words, David went to battle supported by a God-saturated mind. That was his powerful armament. Therefore he knew no fear. And therefore he was victorious.

Now, don't just read that famous Bible passage as an old story, as an exciting bit of ancient history. The idea is to apply its truth to yourself. What are the fearsome problems that confront you, that frighten you, that give you a sense of inadequacy? Stand up to them, as the story says, in the name of the Lord. Almighty God meant us to walk the earth as men and women made in His image, not to crawl through life on our hands and knees.

Select one of those problems that loom so large in your mind and take some action against it. Remember what Emerson said: "Do the thing you fear, and the death of fear is certain." Suppose you're afraid to ask the boss for a raise. Summon up your courage and ask him if you honestly think you deserve it. You may not get it, but you will have done wonders for yourself anyway, because you will have broken through the fear barrier. And that is of more value than a larger paycheck.

Once we had in this country a great psychologist named William James. He pointed out that there is in all of us a psychological barrier that he called the first layer of fatigue. He said that most of us work and struggle until we come to this point and then we say, "I'm so tired. I haven't any more energy. I'll have to stop." But James said that beyond this barrier of fatigue there is tremendous power and energy waiting for us, if we will just force ourselves through it. "The people who really do great things in this world," said William James, "are those who drive past the first layer of fatigue."

Self-doubt is like that, too. It sets up a barrier and timid people turn back when they encounter it. They keep turning back until it becomes a habit—a bad habit. But if you crash through it, if you *make* yourself ask the boss for that raise, if you *do* the thing you fear—just once—the barrier will be broken and your image of yourself will be upgraded. Confidence will begin to flood into your mind and drive out the doubts and the feelings of inadequacy.

There is another thing you can do, too. Examine the life-style you are leading and, if necessary, clean it up. One big cause of inferiority feelings—perhaps the greatest—is wrongdoing, being off the beam from a moral standpoint. People do things that are morally wrong, sometimes because they are tempted, sometimes simply because they want to and think they can get away with it. To use the old-fashioned hard-hitting term, they commit sin. And this is one of the stupidest things you can do, because once you commit a sin it will never let up on you. You can try to ignore it. You can try to put it out of your mind. But it's like putting erroneous information into a computer. It's there. It is not going to disappear. It is going to cause the computer to give wrong answers because it is *programmed* wrong.

A Splinter in the Unconscious

I've never understood why the consequences of sin aren't glaringly obvious to everyone. A moral transgression is like a splinter in the unconscious mind. Unless that splinter is removed, it is going to fester. And what form does this festering take? First of all, it damages the self-esteem of the individual. He knows he has done something wrong, and so he doesn't like himself quite as much as he did before. Next, it begins to affect his performance in subtle but unmistakable ways. A deep, unacknowledged sense of guilt, a built-in censor, will tell that person that so far he may have been doing pretty well, but now, because he has done wrong, he doesn't deserve to do so well anymore. The voice of conscience, the censor within the mind, will say, "You are a wrongdoer, my friend, you are a sinner." It may even get inelegant and say, "You are a dirty dog and you deserve to be punished...and if no one else will punish you, I hereby order you to punish yourself."

Sometimes the punishment is quite subtle in that it takes the form of inefficiency or loss of creativity. Sometimes it appears as ill health. Most often it reveals itself as a growing feeling of inadequacy and inferiority. So if such feelings trouble you, perhaps it would be a good idea to take a ruthless moral inventory of yourself and if necessary change

some area of your life that you may find is not as it should
be.

One last suggestion: If you feel inadequate, sometimes
it is a good idea to ask yourself, "Inadequate compared to
what?" I've known people who were despondent and down-
cast because they allowed themselves to become victims of
too-great expectations. A young man about to enter college
sought me out to talk about his inferiority feelings. It didn't
take much perception to see that the trouble lay in his relationship with his father, or rather, with his father's memory, since the parent had died some years before. The father
had been a great athlete, an all-American fullback, in fact,
and foolishly the boy's mother was forever reminding him
of this. The boy himself simply didn't have the physique
to be a football player, or an outstanding athlete of any kind.
But instead of accepting this fact, he was letting it make
him miserable.

"Look," I said to him after I had asked a few questions.
"You're a good student—probably better than your father
was. You're a fine chess player. You've been the editor of
your high-school yearbook. You're not an inferior person;
you're a superior one. You're just using the wrong yardstick,
that's all! Be proud of your father, sure. But also be proud
of yourself, because you deserve to be!"

Nine times out of ten, as was the case with this youngster,
a feeling of inferiority is nothing but a state of mind. It was
Milton who wrote:

> The mind is its own place, and in itself
> Can make a Heav'n of Hell, a hell of Heav'n.

Image yourself as a worthwhile person; *act as if* you
were someone worthy of admiration and respect—and gradually that is what you will come to be. What you can image,
you will be, in the long run.

To sum up, then, here are some specific things to do if
you need to bolster a shaky ego: Hold in your mind the
image of the kind of person you want to be: confident,
assured, competent, calm. Break through the "fear barrier"
by deliberately doing something that has been causing you

apprehension. Say to yourself, "I can do all things through Christ who strengthens me, and I *will* do this thing that I have been flinching from."

When feelings of inadequacy get you down, remind yourself that God made you and that He does not do poor work. Get rid of such thoughts by seeing yourself as opening up your mind and letting the clean winds of faith blow through. Vividly visualize those winds sweeping away all the cobwebs of self-doubt and self-distrust.

Try to find the root cause of your feelings of inadequacy. Once you bring it into the open, it will lose much of its power to dominate you. Invite the good Lord into your everyday experience. Ask Him to go back into your past, to find the hurtful memories and heal them. He stands ready, always, to aid you.

Turn your sense of inadequacy into a plus by letting it act as a spur, as a motivator. Something in you is yearning and straining to dominate and eliminate weakness. Let the "big you" brush aside the "little you." Visualize the "big you" wielding a big broom and doing just that.

Be realistic; accept some limitations as natural and inevitable. Nobody is "the best" at everything. But image yourself as the best at something.

Stop telling yourself that you can't. Image yourself succeeding in the area where you wish most completely for success. Imagine a television screen on the wall in front of you. In that screen, see yourself as the principal actor doing the thing you long to do. Run this "film" over and over again in your mind. This is the technique that Roger Ferger used, that Mary Crowe used, that Harry DeCamp used, and it is the technique Ruth and I learned in the formation of *Guideposts* magazine.

It is called imaging. It worked for them. It worked for us. It can work for you.

5
How to Manage Money Problems

At a business convention, after I had given a talk that included some of these ideas about the importance and effectiveness of imaging, a man came up and confronted me with a certain truculence. "Well, doctor," he said, "all that stuff about imaging is interesting, but I don't see how it can solve my problem."

Naturally, I asked him what his problem was.

"Money!" he said, "Or rather, lack of money. I'm up to my ears in debt. I have two notes coming due at the bank and I don't know how I'm going to meet either one of them. Will imaging put twenty thousand dollars into my checking account by next Monday? Will imaging take care of my mortgage payments and my insurance payments? Will imaging pay for my wife's new car or my daughter's debut? Come on, be honest now. Yes or no!"

"That's easy," I said. "The answer is no. Imaging isn't some kind of Aladdin's lamp that you can rub and have a genie appear and bring you instant riches."

"Then what good is it to me?" he demanded triumphantly.

"It could do you a lot of good," I told him. "From what

you say, being in debt is a way of life with you. But obviously it's not a way of life that makes you happy. If you would picture yourself debt free with intensity and sincerity, if you would visualize vividly the happiness and peace of mind that solvency would bring you, if you would really make that your aim and give it top priority, you'd move toward that goal and finally achieve it. And *that* would be the result of imaging."

He gave me a strange look, half-skeptical, half-wistful. "You mean," he said, "I should try to see myself managing these money problems—*and* my extravagant wife, *and* my spoiled daughter—instead of having them manage me?"

"Something like that," I told him.

"Thanks," he said. "Maybe I'll give it a try." And he was gone.

I don't know whether that man will be able to upgrade his life-control factor and straighten out his situation, but I do know this: With the possible exception of health problems, money problems weigh more heavily on people's minds than any other form of anxiety. Ruth and I are constantly made aware of this by the mail that reaches us. Despairing letters from elderly people whose fixed incomes are being eroded by inflation. Frantic letters from young people caught in the quicksand of installment buying or credit-card spending. Panicky letters from people staggering under mountainous debts. Fear-filled letters from people who have lost their jobs. The list goes on and on.

Tremendous emotional currents often swirl around money problems. A letter came in the other day from a young woman who said bitterly that she hated money. She hated it for what it did to people like herself who didn't have enough (she'd been laid off from her automotive-company job). She hated it for what she claimed it often did to people who had too much. She said that America had become a materialistic, money-grubbing, dollar-worshipping society, and she blamed money for that. She even misquoted the Bible. "Money is the root of all evil," she wrote, underscoring every word. (Actually, the Bible says that the *love* of money is the root of all evil, quite a different thing.)

As is our custom, Ruth and I discussed the letter and

how to reply to it. Often we turn to the Bible as a guide, or play a kind of game in which each of us reminds the other of a passage that may be pertinent. In this case, we recalled various New Testament references to money, such as the widow's mite. or the thirty pieces of silver paid to Judas.

"It's easy to think of the widow's mite as being good money," Ruth said, "or the money paid to Judas as bad money. But actually money itself is neither good nor bad. It's what people do with it that counts."

"It can symbolize things, though," I said. "In the parable of the talents, for instance, it symbolizes both energetic risk taking and timorous overcaution."

"The *people* in the parable were either energetic or over-cautious," my practical wife said. "Not the money. So hating money, as this woman does, makes about as much sense as hating a stick or a rock!"

In the end I wrote to the young woman and urged her to try to change her image of herself. "Stop seeing yourself as the helpless victim of an imaginary villain called money," I wrote. "If you personalize money s vehemently and hate it so intensely, you certainly won't attract it, because your unconscious mind will be programmed to repel and reject it."

I urged her to create and focus on the self-image of a well-balanced, intelligent person whose mind was able to take change of her emotions. "Calm down," I wrote. "Be objective. Stop all this hate business. Hold the image of yourself as someone determined to remove all these churning, turbulent, conflicting, confusing emotions from your mind. Nothing is going to go right for you until you do."

Anger is just one emotion that money problems can generate. Another is fear. Not long ago I was on a radio show, a call-in program where listeners could pick up the phone and ask questions of the person on the show. One woman who called said to me, "I wish you'd tell me what to do about bill collectors. I'm terrified of them. When a bill collector comes around, I get so nervous and full of fear that I can barely talk to him."

Bill Collectors Are Human, Too

"Well," I said to her, "I happen to know a couple of bill collectors and both have told me how nervous *they* are when they come to a home to talk about nonpayment of bills. They say they get tense and tongue-tied and hot and cold all over."

The woman said, "I can't believe it!"

"It's true," I told her. "A bill collector is also a human being and is not trying to harass you or be mean to you or put you in jail. He's just representing a man or woman in business who has to get money to keep on selling merchandise to people like yourself. He wants you to continue to be a paying customer, so he wants you to stay solvent. His main objective is to get you to work out a payment plan.

"So here's a suggestion. The next time a bill collector comes to your door, change the picture you have in your mind of what the interview is going to be like. Instead of seeing yourself as embarrassed and angry and evasive, and him as hostile and threatening, visualize a meeting between a nice person who has a job to do and a nice person who happens to have some unpaid bills. See both of you working out a solution together in a friendly way. And here's another suggestion: Before you open the door, say a quick prayer for the poor fellow, because he's probably just as nervous as you are."

"Well," she said, "I certainly never thought of praying for a bill collector. But if you say so, I'll try."

In trying to solve life's problems, imaging is only one of the many techniques. Through the years, trying to help people in financial difficulty, Ruth and I have worked out half a dozen simple suggestions that seem to be effective.

The first is simply this: *don't panic*. If you find anxiety getting the upper hand, go to work imaging peace of mind. The simple act of praying creates an image of your problems being brought to the Source of all wisdom, and that is tremendously reassuring and comforting. Then read the

Twenty-third Psalm. When you come to those marvelous words "...I will fear no evil: for thou art with me..." (verse 4), run them through your mind at least twenty times. Repeat them to yourself during the day if you feel your anxiety returning. Write them on a piece of paper and tape it on your bathroom mirror, where you will see it first thing every morning. Saturate yourself with this idea.

Then, when you have your emotions under control, the next step is to *get organized*. This is Ruth's favorite bit of advice because she is a highly organized person herself. Make a complete list of all your debts, everything you owe. Make another list of essential expenses. Add up all sources of income and see what you can count on. It's amazing how many people really don't know exactly how much they owe or what their basic expenses are. Visualize yourself living within your income with a fraction left over for debt reduction. Paint that image vividly in your mind.

Next, *be disciplined*. You have to learn to ignore that sly little destructive demon named Instant Gratification who lurks in all of us and whispers, "That's pretty; get it!" or, "That's a bargain; grab it!"

The demon is happiest when you don't know the true state of your finances, because then he knows you are less likely to apply the brakes. I must confess that's one of the problems Ruth and I had to work through in the early years of our marriage. Soon after we moved to New York, I decided that we had to have a new car. The old one was falling apart and beginning to cost a lot of money in repairs. So I went to a car showroom, picked out one I liked, and told the salesman to hold it for me.

When I told Ruth about it that night, she shook her head. "No," she said.

"What do you mean, 'No'?" I asked her.

She said, "I mean, we can't afford it. Our budget barely takes care of things now. There's no money for new-car payments. So forget it!"

Well, naturally, this reduced me to a state of gloom, especially when I had to call up and disappoint the eager salesman. But Ruth was applying precisely the ingredient—

discipline—that fends off money problems before they can get started.

A fourth suggestion we sometimes offer is blunt and to the point: *think*. If you'll just sit down and really think, you may come up with an idea or an insight that can change everything.

I've always liked William Saroyan's story about the time when, as a struggling young writer, discouraged and almost broke, he decided to ask a rich uncle in a nearby city for a loan. With his last bit of cash, Saroyan sent his uncle a telegram. Back came a reply of just three words: HAVE HEAD EXAMINED.

Once he got over the shock of this seemingly sardonic refusal, Saroyan pondered the message. Gradually he began to see what his uncle was saying: You don't need a loan. Look inside your head. That's where you'll find a solution in a new idea.

Thus challenged, Saroyan sat down, thought up a plot for a short story, wrote it, sold it, and was on his way to a brilliant career as a playwright and novelist.

There's Always an Answer

Remember my druggist friend, A.E. Russ, who told me not to worry about an occasional inept sermon? He had a niece who was living in upstate New York when the crash of the big depression came. Her husband lost his business. Things went from bad to worse. Finally Russ decided to go up to Utica and see if he could be of any help to them.

He found his niece and her husband dejected and disheartened. All they could talk about was the depression and the grim things that had happened to them. But Uncle Alfred refused to join them in their gloomy postmortems. "Let's focus on the future," he said. "Find something to build on. Let's go over *everything* with the future in mind. Forget the past. Think of the future!"

As they talked, he noticed that his niece was sewing something, and he asked her what it was. She told him that it was just a pot holder.

"Very pretty," he said. "Do you have any more?"

She said she had made a dozen or so.

"Well," said Uncle Alfred, "they're *good* pot holders— a lot better than most. So why don't you take them down to Woolworth's tomorrow and see their buyer. He might order some."

The niece was hesitant and her husband skeptical, but Uncle Alfred was firm. "Let's do some practical imaging. There is going to be a factory someday," he said. "A factory making pot holders and all sorts of other useful things. I can see it right now in my mind: tall chimneys, employees streaming through a gate in a big fence, an enormous sign with your name on it. Now you just go down to Woolworth's, keeping that thought in mind, and see what happens!"

Years later, I happened to be in a Pullman car early one morning on my way back to New York from a speaking engagement. Approaching Utica, I pulled up the shade in my lower berth and looked out. The train was passing a sizable textile factory with a tall fence and a sign at least twenty feet high. And you can guess whose name was on the sign! Why? Because in this case someone, Uncle Alfred, "had his head examined," did some creative imaging, and found a simple solution to a massive problem.

One more example. Soon after World War II a young man named Hal LeMaster went to Florida to seek his fortune. Nothing much happened until one day when he was alone, fishing for trout. Nearby was a boat with an old man who kept hauling in fish while LeMaster had no bites at all. When LeMaster asked plaintively how he did it, the old fellow explained that he was using live sardines, little silvery minnows, for bait. "The trout see 'em flash," he said. "They can't see the bait you're using."

LeMaster went home, shaped an artificial minnow out of transparent plastic, added hooks, and put a strip of shiny metal inside. Result: the famed "Mirro-lure" that became a national favorite and made LeMaster a rich man—all because he "had his head examined"—by himself!

Opportunities for moneymaking surround us all the time; it just takes an inquisitive, lively mind to see them. It also takes an optimistic mind, one that expects good things to happen in the future.

It's not easy to stay optimistic these days because pessimism is so rampant. Newspapers are full of it. So are the airwaves. One night Ruth and I were watching a television program about the troubles of a young farmer and his family. This man had a small farm with a few cows and some chickens. But he had run out of cash and stumbled into debt, and now his creditors were going to take away his cows as payment for those debts. He was probably going to lose his house, too, we were told. He wasn't eligible for welfare, apparently, because he still owned some livestock. His three children were reduced to eating sandwiches, and the gloomy thought was introduced that pretty soon there might be no more sandwiches.

Now here was a genuine case of economic hardship, but the whole thrust of that presentation was to tell millions of viewers that the way to handle a money problem is to add up and focus on and dwell upon all the difficulties involved.

Ruth said impatiently, "This is all so downbeat! Why doesn't someone tell those people to make a list of their remaining assets? That might give them the kind of lift they need."

"What assets would you list?" I asked, just to see what she would say.

"Well," she said, "the man seems healthy and strong, a vigorous person. That's asset number one. Next, he has a wife who seems intelligent, who obviously loves him and is loyal to him. That's asset number two. The kids are not crippled or sick or handicapped in any way; they're normal, healthy kids. So that's asset number three. He hasn't lost his house yet; they still have a roof over their heads. That's asset number four. Their plight is being brought to the attention of millions of sympathetic Americans, some of whom will undoubtedly try to help them. That's asset number five. But nobody even mentions these things!"

On the contrary, while we continued to watch, the commentator went on to say dolefully that the young farmer had been reduced to taking on odd jobs.

"Reduced?" I said to Ruth. "What is so reducing about an odd job? Remember Michael Cardone?"

Michael Cardone is a friend of ours who in middle age found himself out of work. But he didn't let it get him down. One day he saw a pile of discarded, worn-out windshield-wiper motors in a garage, and he began to wonder why they couldn't be fixed and sold more cheaply than new ones. So he began to fix them and sell them—a pretty odd job because there was no demand for rebuilt wiper motors and no one had ever bothered to do it before. But he kept on, and today Michael Cardone is the head of an enormous plant in Philadelphia that makes all sorts of automotive supplies. Why? Because he had a dream, an image of being his own boss, of running his own show, of finding automotive needs and filling them—and an odd job was the springboard that started him on his way. And what he was able to image, he became.

Michael Cardone is an intensely religious man. He and the top executives in his company begin every business day with prayer. They're convinced that if they have God as their senior partner, and make all decisions in the light of His teachings, they cannot go wrong. Michael himself is sure that there is a spiritual side to every great success story, and his own accomplishments seem to prove him right.

Ruth and I agree with Michael in believing that there is a spiritual force in all this, something that goes beyond the reach of reason. A woman once said to me, a bit snappishly, when I was trying to help her overcome her fears about money problems, "What do you know about what I'm going through? You're a successful minister, a well-known personality, a writer of books, publisher of *Guideposts*, a popular magazine. You don't have any debts. You don't owe anybody anything. You're not afraid somebody may show up any minute to turn off your electricity or repossess your secondhand car. So how can you understand what I'm going through?"

I said to her, "I can understand it because I've been through it, too. You're too young to remember the Great Depression, but I do, and believe me, it makes all these recent 'recessions' look like Sunday-school picnics."

I told her that back in 1930 I was a young minister, recently married, in Syracuse, New York. My salary, which had been a handsome (for those days) six thousand dollars a year, was cut twice—first to five thousand, then to four thousand. We had no manse or home supplied by the church. Everyone was frightened and depressed. Businesses were failing. Nobody could borrow money; there was no money to be had. Men used to greet one another grimly by saying, "Have you had your pay cut yet?" Everyone had to take several cuts before that depression ended, and many people lost their jobs altogether.

At four thousand dollars a year, I just didn't see how we could get by. My salary was the only income we had. I was helping my younger brother with college expenses and I knew he had to count on that. The pressure got worse and worse. I hated to burden Ruth with my fears. One night I went out alone and walked through Walnut Park near our little apartment, and for the first time in my life I felt icy terror clutching at my mind and heart. I wasn't just worried; I was terrified. When I finally went home, I could keep it to myself no longer. I said to Ruth, "We're in a desperate situation. We can't pay the bills. What are we going to do?" And her answer really startled me. She said, "We're going to start tithing."

Our Financial Problem Solved

"Tithing?" I echoed. "Tithing with what? We can't do it. It's impossible!"

"No," Ruth said. "Not impossible. Essential. You know what the Bible promises to those who give ten percent of everything to the Lord." I can see her yet, standing right there in the kitchen and quoting Malachi 3:10 to me: "Bring ye all the tithes into the storehouse... and prove me now herewith, saith the Lord of hosts, if I will not open you the windows of heaven, and pour you out a blessing, that there shall not be room enough to receive it."

"We're going to do that," she said stoutly, "and we're not going to starve either. We're not going to be evicted.

We are going to get by on ninety percent of your twice-cut salary because tithing is an act of faith, and the Bible says that if we have faith even as small as a grain of mustard seed, nothing will be impossible for us. We have to start imaging God's prosperity."

So we did it. And Ruth was right, we did get by. Money certainly didn't pour in, but there always was just enough. Furthermore, the act of tithing seemed to calm my fears and stimulate my mind so that I began thinking. I started imaging. I knew I had one small talent: public speaking. And so I decided to try to capitalize on that. I offered myself as a public speaker wherever one was needed. I spoke at civic clubs and garden clubs and graduations and community gatherings. Sometimes I was paid five or ten dollars, sometimes nothing at all. But it helped. What a thrill I felt when I received the first twenty-five dollar fee. Then someone who heard me speak offered me a chance to go on radio. Again, there was no money for this, but the number of speaking invitations increased. So one thing led to another, and gradually we began to get our heads above water.

I am convinced that tithing did it. Anyway, Ruth and I have been tithers ever since, and there is something about this practice of giving that can't be explained in purely rational terms. Tithing seems to put a person in touch with some mysterious force that attracts money. Not a lot of money, necessarily, but enough for the tither's needs. Through the years, in sermons and talks I have recommended tithing to thousands of people, and hundreds have been persuaded to try it. Of those hundreds, not one has ever come back to me and said that the experiment failed, or that he regretted it, or that it was a mistake. Not a single one.

It's almost as if there were an invisible reservoir of abundance in the universe that can be tapped if you will just obey certain spiritual laws. The word *abundance*, I'm told, comes from a Latin phrase meaning to "rise up in waves." When you tithe, it does seem as if little waves of abundance start rising up all around you.

So if you have financial difficulties, face up to them not

just with courage and intelligence but also with warmhearted generosity and concern for others.

Here, then, are the key things to remember where money problems are concerned:

1. *Don't panic*. Fear not only paralyzes the will and the mind but it also seems, in some mysterious way, to scare money away, probably because fearful people are not creative or resourceful people. So try to be calm, be objective, be logical, be hopeful.

2. *Get organized*. Figure out exactly what your income is and what your outlays are. If you can't increase the former, reduce the latter until your budget is in balance. That's the only way to get runaway finances under control.

3. *Be disciplined*. Don't be an impulse buyer. Give up all credit or installment buying until you are debt free.

4. *Think*. Look inside your head for new ideas, new possible sources of income. Money problems can become assets if they force you into creative thinking. You may strike a vein of gold, as Michael Cardone did, that will last for the rest of your life.

5. *Give all you can*. Giving is the best way to put yourself in the great invisible stream of abundance that surges through the universe. Tithing is the surest way to do this, because God Himself has guaranteed the results, and God's promises never fail.

6. *Visualize yourself as debt free*. Imagine vividly the relief, the happiness, the peace of mind you will feel when the last payment is made. Hold that idea in your conscious mind until it sinks down into your unconscious mind. And then you will have it forever, because it will have you.

6
Use Imaging to Outwit Worry

One never knows exactly what kind of spark will set a man on fire. I once knew a salesman whose life seemed to exhibit a consistent pattern of failure. He was worried, low on cash, and very low in spirit. He would try selling one thing and then another. One season it would be paint and the next cosmetics and the next office supplies and the next lamps and furniture. But no matter what commodity he was offering, he never seemed to make a success of it, and the image of failure became stamped more and more indelibly on his mind.

Then one day someone handed him a piece of paper with a three-line affirmation on it. It went like this:

> I believe that I am always divinely
>   guided.
> I believe that I will always take the right
>   turn in the road.
> I believe that God will make a way where
>   there is no way.

Three lines. Nothing very complicated. No great eloquence. Rather repetitious, in fact. But this salesman began repeating these lines to himself every morning when he first woke up and every night when he went to bed. He memorized them. He let them sink deep into his innermost consciousness. And gradually this man began to change.

He no longer dithered and hesitated over what items he would try to sell. In his simple and unquestioning way he asked God to tell him. Then he listened, believingly, for an answer, meanwhile thanking God in advance for giving him the right answer. When he seemed to feel a nudge in the direction of one item or another, he chose it without hesitation and did not look back. He believed that he was divinely guided, so his choice could not be a mistake. Therefore, when he began to sell the item, he did so with complete conviction that that was the item he *should* be selling—and that his customers would be buying.

If he had to choose between two different cities or two different territories, he went through the same procedure. He asked God to show him the right turn in the road and he thanked God in advance for so guiding him. Then when he felt a nudge in one direction or the other, he followed it without hesitation and without looking back. He was positive that it was the right choice.

If he ran into sales resistance or if a hoped-for sale did not materialize, he didn't become discouraged. He believed that God would make a way where there was no way. His attitude of quiet assurance was so impresive that prospective customers felt it and reacted favorably to it. There was something about the salesman now that inspired great confidence, whereas before he had seemed so uncertain and unsure of himself that prospective customers felt unsure about him.

This dramatic change in personality and approach was accompanied by an equally dramatic change in the image the salesman had of himself. Formerly he had visualized failure and defeat before he even set out on the road. And failure and defeat were what he invariably found. Now he imaged himself succeeding because his conscious mind *and* his unconscious mind had accepted the belief that with God as his ally and partner, he could not fail. Once he began to act as if he could not fail, he did not fail. Before each scheduled road trip was over, he had sold all his stock and had to come home to replenish it. He went on to become one of the best salesmen in his part of the country, all because his life had been revolutionized by three simple phrases, each beginning with two magic words: *I believe*.

But there is also such a thing as negative imaging. And the most common name for it is worry. When we worry we are using imaging, all right, but we are pointing it in the wrong direction. When we worry about our health, or our children, or our jobs, or our future, we are giving these fears a degree of reality by allowing them to pervade and color our thinking. And if they dominate our minds, they may also affect our actions. Just as affirmative imaging tends to actualize desirable events sooner or later, so negative imaging, or worry, tends to create conditions in which the unpleasant thing that is worried about has a better chance of coming to pass.

The Bible, that extraordinary Book of Wisdom, clearly recognizes this. In the Book of Job, perhaps the most ancient of all biblical writings, Job cries plaintively: "The thing which I greatly feared is come upon me . . ." (Job 3:25). Of course it did. He imaged this dire happening. He *greatly* feared something, and finally it happened. Haven't you known of cases yourself where people display excessive fears of some misfortune and then that misfortune seems to seek them out? I know I have.

The Bible never mentions a problem without offering a solution. There are constant exhortations to cheerfulness, to hope, to faith—all tested antidotes to worry. "A merry heart doeth good like a medicine" (Proverbs 17:22). "Say to them that are of a fearful heart, Be strong, fear not" (Isaiah 35:4). ". . . my peace I give unto you" (John 14:27). Trust God, the Bible keeps saying, because the more you trust the less you will have to worry about.

Let's be realistic: anyone who has any imagination at all is going to be concerned now and then. A little worry is probably a good thing, if it impels a person to take prudent action. It's chronic worry that is dangerous, the *constant* imaging of undesirable events. The occasional worrier takes affirmative action. The chronic worrier becomes exhausted and confused, like a desert traveler in a swirling sandstorm. His friends may say to him, "Why don't you stop worrying? It's just a waste of time. Doesn't change a thing!" But usually he is unable to follow this cheery advice. And as a matter of fact, that last phrase is dangerously misleading because worry *does* change things—mainly the capacity of the worrier to cope successfully with the thing that is worrying him.

When worry becomes really acute, it can clamp down on the mind like a vise, blotting out all rational thought processes. This is how black magic works. A friend of mine who lives in South Africa once told me how his mother's maid became convinced that a local witch doctor had put a spell on her because she had offended him in some manner. She became unable to eat because all food seemed to have a terrible odor, although actually it didn't. Everything edible became repulsive to her. She was convinced that she was going to die, and although her employers called in doctors and ministers to help her, she finally did die of starvation— so powerful were the negative images that had taken possession of her mind.

A year or two ago, when I was on a national radio program in Australia, a similar situation was brought to my attention. A young girl, a member of one of the aboriginal tribes, was near death because she, too, was convinced that she was the victim of a spell. In this case, when asked if positive thinking might help, I said that the power of faith was stronger than any so-called occult power, and I called upon the radio audience to join me in a massive prayer effort for the girl's deliverance. I suggested that everyone image her as being set free from the deadly idea that was killing her. I think a lot of listeners did, because later I heard that the spell was broken; the girl began to eat again and eventually regained her health.

Few of us ever encounter such dramatic evidences of the power of fear or worry to produce such deadly images, but most of us do have to struggle with worry on a day-to-day basis. And even in relatively mild doses, it can be painful.

The word *worry* itself comes from an old Anglo-Saxon term meaning to choke, or strangle, and that is exactly what worry does—it chokes the joy of living right out of its victim. And it chokes off creative power to improve one's condition.

How, then, does one get rid of the clammy, clutching hands of worry around one's neck? How does one let go of worry thoughts, with their bleak images of future problems or disasters lurking just around the next bend in the road?

Believe Worry Can Be Overcome

In the first place, you must believe it can be done. This is the same as saying, picture or image yourself as worry free, and have faith that that picture can become a reality. Worry is a habit. It got into your mind because you *practiced* it, and anything you practice in, you can practice out.

How did you first develop the habit of worrying? It probably began as a thin trickle of negative imaging across your mind. Then, repeated many times, it cut a channel into your consciousness. If this process is not checked, eventually every thought you think may be drained into this channel of worry and come up so tinctured that you see everything in terms that are dark and foreboding.

There is something obscurely satisfying, or shall we say sort of masochistic, about worrying that makes the habit hard to break. Just as some people "enjoy poor health," so some people seem to enjoy worrying in a miserable sort of way. More than once I have suggested to my congregation how wonderful it would be if they could just come forward to the altar, put their worries into a large basket or other receptacle, and leave them there. "But then, you know," I sometimes add, "after the service some of you would creep back down the aisle and fish around in the basket until you found your discarded worry. You'd gotten so fond of it that you couldn't bear to be without it. And you'd go out hugging it tightly to you because you couldn't part with such an old, familiar friend." This always gets a laugh, or at least a chuckle, from my listeners. But there's more than a grain of truth in it, and they know it.

Let me give you a few tips that have helped me outwit worry.

First, if you have something preying on your mind (good phrase; that's exactly what worry does), *think* about it. Stop imaging the worst possible eventuality and reacting with fear and dread and apprehension. Push aside these negative emotions and use your mind positively. Thought is one of the greatest faculties that God gave to us human beings. I'm convinced that we can control almost anything in our lives by thought. Therefore worry, which is an irrational reaction, can be controlled by thinking rationally. Take a worry apart, lay it out, dissect it, analyze it. If you will do this with clear, cool, rational thinking, you'll find that nine times out of ten there won't be much left. There is so much illusionary content in worry that when this is dispelled, the reality that is left will prove to be very small—so small that you can handle it.

When I was a young man, I had a wise old friend, Dr. David Keppel. I used to seek him out when I was struggling with some problem. "Norman," he would say, "let's sit down and take this thing apart." And remarkably, when he got through doing that, as a rule there wasn't much of anything worrisome left. He always said that ninety-five percent of his own worries either never happened or were relatively innocuous when they did happen. "I could always handle that five percent," he used to say. He even wrote a poem about it that, if my memory serves me, went like this:

> Better never trouble Trouble
> Until Trouble troubles you;
> For you only make your trouble
> Double-trouble if you do;
> And the trouble—like a bubble—
> That you're troubling about,
> May be nothing but a cipher
> With its rim rubbed out.

Another useful way to outwit worry is to use symbolism to get rid of it. This is a form of imaging, of course, and it can be very helpful. Once a woman came to me because she was worried—almost literally—out of her senses. Some months previously she had had a slight heart attack. Her doctors told her she had made a good recovery and that her prospects were excellent, but she was obsessed by the fear of dying at any minute. She talked so compulsively and continuously about this fear that I could not get a word into the conversation. Finally I held out my hand, palm upward, and said, "Put it there."

"Put what there?" she asked, bewildered.

"Your problem," I said. "This things that's worrying you. I know it's invisible, but I also know it's very real. I want you to stretch out your hand and put it into my hand."

Somewhat hesitantly she went through the procedure. I stood up, went to the door, opened it, and made a throwing gesture as if I were casting something out. I closed the door and went back to where she sat. "Now," I said, "the problem is no longer in this room. It's outside that door. We need to deal with it, and we will deal with it. But first we're going to fill the place inside you where that problem was with some thoughts of God and faith and hope. We're going to saturate your mind with the peace that Jesus Christ promised to all of us. And you will find that these thoughts are stronger than worry, stronger than fear."

And eventually she did. But first there had to be the symbolism, or the imaging, that made her receptive.

Many people use this device with good results. A letter came the other day from a woman who said she had been a chronic worrier until she hit upon the device of writing her worries down on slips of paper and putting them in an old teapot that she kept on a high shelf in her kitchen. Every time she put a problem in the pot she said a little prayer, releasing the problem to the Lord. At the end of the year she would take the pot down, read all the slips, and then throw them away. It was amazing, she said, how many of her worries had simply evaporated. And she always felt capable of dealing with the rest.

The late Lord Rank, an outstanding British industrialist, once rather whimsically told me of a little game he played to reduce the impact of worry. He organized what he called the "Wednesday Worry Club." He was the sole member.

Instead of worrying every day, whenever a worry cropped up he would write it on a piece of paper and drop it in a box to be worried about on Wednesday afternoon at four o'clock, the meeting time of the "club."

At that time, he would empty all the deposited worries on a table. In going over them, always about 90 percent had solved themselves and no longer needed to be worried about. "But," I asked, "What did you do with the other ten percent?"

"I put them back in the box to be worried about next Wednesday at four o'clock," blandly replied Lord Rank.

This same wise man told me that there were thirteen steps leading from the courtyard to his office. As he mounted them every morning, it was his custom to say a brief prayer on each step, affirming and giving thanks for the goodness of God. He knew how to outwit worry.

A man I know in Chicago is the treasurer and financial genius of a large corporation. He said to me once, "Would you like to know what I do when I've got worries? When it's time to leave the office for the day, I write them on a piece of paper and put it in my pocket. When I get home I put my car in the garage and walk to our front gate, where there is a mailbox. I open it, put the paper in it, close my eyes, and say, 'Dear Lord, I'm giving You my worries. Work on them for me during the night, will You?' I leave them there, and when I come out in the morning, the problem may still be there, but it's no longer on top of me. Rather, I'm on top of it. What was a source of anxiety the night before has now become an exciting intellectual challenge—and it's amazing how often I find the right answer."

Turn Away From Worry

A third way to break the worry pattern is one that is available to all of us: divert yourself. Our word *diversion* comes from two Latin words meaning to "turn away from," and when worry begins to be a problem, that is the sensible thing to do: simply turn away from it.

This is not hard because fortunately the human mind is

designed so that it cannot hold more than one idea at a time. You cannot actively worry about something when you are deliberately focusing on something else. So when worry has you by the throat, the simplest way to break its grip is to do something that you enjoy doing. Dig in the garden; play a game of golf; arrange some flowers; bake a cake; sing a song (why not a grand old hymn?); take the dog for a run; have lunch with a friend; buy yourself a present; read a good book; go to a decent movie (if you can find one!); plan a trip; browse through a museum; take a child on a picnic. If all else fails, turn on the television! Anything to get your mind off yourself. Robert Louis Stevenson wrote: "The world is so full of a number of things, I'm sure we should all be as happy as kings." The world *is* full of an infinite number of things, but this won't do you much good unless you make a deliberate effort to reach out and include them in your life as worthwhile forms of diversion.

The final and best antidote for worry is simply this: Image Jesus Christ as actually your personal friend. Don't regard Him as some remote, historical, stained-glass kind of figure. Image Him as your constant companion throughout the day. Paint a portrait in your mind of what you think He looks like. Fill in the details: His compassionate eyes, those strong carpenter's hands. How did His voice sound when He talked to people, when He told the story of the Prodigal Son, for example? He must have had a wonderful laugh; can you picture yourself sitting on a hillside in Galilee, hearing it? If you can picture that, why not picture Him sitting alongside of you right now?

The more vivid that image in your mind, the freer from worry you will be. Some years ago a professor of physics from a famous university came to see me. He was a very intelligent man, but haunted by irrational fears and worries that were interfering with his work and making his life miserable. After some discussion, it became evident that the trouble lay in certain immoralities he had committed years earlier. He had asked for forgiveness of those sins, and I was sure it had been granted. But, like many of us, he had not forgiven himself, and his worries and his sense of inferiority and inadequacy came from these deep guilt feelings.

I decided to suggest something that I had used successfully with people of less formidable education. I didn't know how he would react, but my suggestion was that every night, upon going to bed, he place a chair beside his bed and tell himself that Jesus was sitting in that chair all night, watching over him and lifting the burden of worry from his shoulders.

As I expected, he looked uncomfortable. "But that sort of fantasy is for children," he protested.

"The Bible tells us to become like little children," I reminded him. "Maybe that is because they are less likely to be doubters. All you need is a grain of faith—one about the size of a mustard seed will do."

Finally he agreed to try it. At the end of two weeks he called me. "I was about ready to give up on that idea of yours," he said. "But two nights ago—well, I can't exactly explain it, but suddenly I knew in some way much deeper than reason that the Lord actually *was* there beside me. I'm sure of it. And I believe the grip that guilt and fear and worry and all that depressing stuff had on me is broken. For the first time in years, I actually feel set free."

And subsequently he found that he was, for a fact, free! That was why Christ came into the world, so we are told—to free captives like my physicist friend. And anyone, including you, can be free of worry if you will fill your mind with the factual idea that God is with you and is giving you a normal, steady, intelligent attitude toward the problems of life. When you image yourself as living close to God, you will have the ability to get your mind above the confusion and heat of worry into a place of clarity and calm. Many have found this practice the best way to outwit worry.

Imaging outwits worry. Try it. You'll see.

7
Image Yourself
No Longer Lonely

An unhappy woman came to consult me a few months ago. She was in her mid-fifties, I judged, pleasant looking but with an aura of dejection about her. "Dr. Peale," she said. "I'm in prison, and I can't get out."

"What sort of prison?" I asked her.

"The prison of loneliness," she said. "The prison of isolation from life. And I'm not the only one; there are thousands upon thousands of us—mostly elderly people, but some just middle-aged and widowed, like me. Solitary human beings living in the loneliest solitude of all—the solitude of a big city."

She looked down at the handkerchief she was twisting in her fingers. Finally she went on: "The days crawl by, one just like another. And do you know what the worst time of all is? It's 6:00 P.M. That is when Ralph used to come home from the office, and we would have an hour or so together before I'd get dinner on the table. I used to wait for the sound of his key in the lock of our apartment. Now six o'clock comes, and there is no key in the lock, no familiar face, no one to prepare a meal for. I turn on the six o'clock news and look at it, but I don't really hear it, because I'm so lonely I just want to die."

I did feel sorry for her. I said, "Don't you have some friends or relatives who can partially fill the gap left by your husband's death?"

She shook her head. "No relatives here in the city," she said. "My two daughters are married and live elsewhere. I have a few acquaintances, but they are all busy with their own lives. They don't have time for me, and I don't blame them."

"Why do you say that?" I asked her.

"Well," she said with a wan smile, "I'm not the most scintillating company in the world. I never finished college; I just met Ralph and married him. I don't have much to contribute, I guess. I don't have any skills to get a job with. I'm just a homebody, really. Nobody cares much about homebodies these days."

"You say you're a prisoner," I said to her. "And you want me to help you organize a jailbreak. Well, to begin with, do you know who holds the key to your cell? Do you know who your jailer really is?"

"No," she said, looking puzzled, "not really."

"I think you do know," I told her. "The jailer is you. You're the only person who has the key to your cell. You're the only one who can open the door that leads to freedom. You'll never do it so long as you hold in your mind this image of yourself as a helpless victim of circumstance, a woman who lacks friends because she thinks she has so little to contribute, a person hopelessly trapped in a dungeon of loneliness. If you continue to image yourself that way, that is what you will continue to be. So if we are really going to organize a jailbreak, we will have to begin with you and some of these attitudes that are walling you in."

"Isn't it too late," she said, "to start changing attitudes at my age?"

"That is just the sort of attitude we need to change," I told her. "Of course it's not too late! We can start right now. We are going to do some creative imaging of a fascinating existence for you. You said you see yourself as a prisoner—lonely, almost friendless, living in a drab procession of monotonous days where nothing ever happens. Now I challenge you, this very moment, to throw that tired, old, downbeat, negative image of yourself right out of your mind. In its place visualize a woman—you—with a smile on her face and a song in her heart, inviting a friend over for lunch or a movie or a trip to a museum—and being invited back, taking bridge lessons, perhaps, until she becomes a good player, offering her time and energy as a volunteer at some hospital, buying a new dress or a new coat, going to church on Sunday and meeting new people, taking up a new hobby or two, photography, perhaps, birdwatching, anything. But always image a new life, a vital, interesting life."

I was watching her face as I talked, and I could see hope and doubt simultaneously in her eyes.

Image the New You

"Push those doubts out of your mind, and do it now," I told her. "Pin up this image of the new you that I'm giving you in their place. The doubts will try to come back, and so will a lot of other old, tired attitudes and habits. You just have to practice *dis*placing everything that contributes to a poor self-image and *re*placing those things with realizable goals. What I'm portraying is not beyond your reach. It is a personality change that you can have if you make up your mind to have it, if you desire it with all your heart, if you pray for help in obtaining it. Start every day with a prayer. Prayerize, visualize, actualize—that is the formula for successful imaging. If you carry out the first two steps with all the intensity you can muster, I promise you that the third step will take care of itself."

Twice since then, I've had occasional reports from this woman. She hasn't turned into a complete extrovert overnight, but she is really trying and she is getting somewhere with her new self-image. She is busier and she is happier—and she's stopped thinking of herself as a prisoner. She said that whenever she feels the old insidious chill of loneliness beginning to creep back into her life, she picks up the phone and calls someone who may be lonelier than she is. So I have no doubt that she will conquer her loneliness, because she has discovered the best solution of all: thinking about other people instead of herself.

I've heard it said that loneliness is the great modern plague, that it exists in epidemic proportions. Well, let's take a closer look at this affliction that claims so many victims, and try to list some countermeasures.

First, I think it helps to realize that being alone doesn't necessarily make you lonely. I know quite a few people who actually enjoy solitude because they've mastered the art of living pleasantly with themselves.

Some lucky people seem to be born with this happy faculty. One night when our daughter Margaret was about four years old I heard her laughing and talking to herself long after she should have been asleep. I went into her room and asked her what was going on. "Oh," she said, "I'm just laughing because I have such a good time with me!" And I remember thinking. *What a wonderful way to be.* You have to spend every minute of your life in your own company. If you don't enjoy it, you're going to be miserable. If you do enjoy it, solitude will never bother you.

If the time you spend alone is to be spent pleasantly, you have to know yourself—and you have to like yourself.

Knowing yourself means understanding what makes you happy, what makes you sad, what gives you pleasure, and what bores you. Take myself, for example: I'm a worker. I like to work, I am accustomed to work, I feel happiest when I'm working. Holidays tend to make me restless because I have the uncomfortable feeling that I'm wasting my time. I like the satisfaction that comes from getting things done, so when I have to be alone I'm able to live pleasantly with myself by filling my waking hours with the work I love to do—like writing this book, for example.

Like Yourself

Then there is the question of liking yourself. Most of us think of ourselves quite favorably most of the time. But there are a surprising number of people whose self-esteem is too low. People who have done things they are ashamed of, or suffer from an inferiority complex, or demand too much of themselves and then blame themselves when they fall short. How can other people be attracted to them if they don't like themselves?

The plain truth is, many lonely people are lonely because they turn other people off. They are irritable. Or rude. Or complaining. Or critical. Or self-centered, Or downbeat. Or opinionated. Or just plain dull.

Sometimes they have little mannerisms that drive you up a wall. Many years ago I knew a woman—a good-hearted person, really—who seemed to walk through life in slow motion. She moved deliberately, she talked deliberately, she thought deliberately. Since she was a member of a committee on which I also served, I had to have lunch with her occasionally. When I did, I almost had to grit my teeth to keep from showing impatience as she *slowly* pushed each morsel of food at least six times around her plate, *slowly* raised it to her mouth, *slowly* chewed and chewed. I was able to endure it, due to infrequent meetings, and I always try to take people as they come. But I learned that others fled her in droves.

So if you are lonely, you must face the possibility that something in your own personality is causing that loneliness. And if it is, you have to isolate it and actively do something about it.

Try to see yourself as others may see you. What sort of expression do you habitually wear? Does a smile come easily, or do you feel more at ease with a frown?

How is your posture? Do you stand straight and tall, or do you slump dejectedly?

Do you project an aura of cheerfulness and confidence, or would you make a perceptive observer say, "Here comes bad news!"

How about your dress and your grooming? Are you an attractive-looking person, someone you yourself would like to meet? What about your conversation? Are most of your opinions enthusiastic and optimistic—or are they the reverse? Do the things you find fault with outnumber the things you praise? How many of your sentences begin with a capital "I"?

Do you truly pay attention to what the other person is saying, or are you too busy thinking about what *you* will say next?

Have you learned the basic rule of successful small talk, which is to inquire about other people's interests, or do you rattle incessantly about your own?

Review your attitude about people in general. Ask yourself honestly: Do you really like to be around people? Do you care about them and show them that you care? When you have an outflowing attitude of genuine caring, it creates a state of harmony between you and other people that is irresistible. People feel it instantly, and they always respond.

Another cure for loneliness lies in that old exhortation: Don't just sit there, do something! One of the most common causes of loneliness is inertia and the apathy that comes from not having enough to do.

I remember one day coming out of a Rotary luncheon and seeing a forlorn woman sitting in the lobby of the hotel. She was the widow of a Rotarian who had died some weeks before. When I asked her why she was there, she said that it made her feel less lonely to sit outside the Rotary meeting that had meant so much to her husband.

"If you'll come with me," I told her, "I'll give you a better solution." I took her to my church, where some cheerful women volunteers were stuffing envelopes and having a lot of fun together. "Here is a new helper," I said to them. "Take her in. Make friends with her. Above all, keep her busy." And they did. She told me afterward that having something useful to do, and congenial people to do it with, had rescued her from despair.

But remember this: If you are lonely, you can't just wait for someone to come along and rescue you. You have to be willing to make a move yourself. Form a picture of the interesting life you want to live and of one in which you have many friends and exciting interests. Hold that image and move constantly toward it. The mental picture will reproduce itself as fact.

The truth is, we all need supportive relationships. I once heard a lecture in which the speaker talked about the great redwood trees of California, those magnificent giants of the forest towering as much as three hundred feet in the air. "You'd think such tall trees would require very deep roots," the speaker said. "Actually, redwoods have a very shallow root system, designed to capture all the surface moisture possible. These roots spread out in all directions, and as a result, all the roots of all the trees in the redwood grove are intertwined. They are locked together so that when the wind blows or a storm strikes, all the trees support and sustain one another. That is why you almost never see a redwood standing alone. They need one another to survive."

Most people do, too.

Finally, the best remedy for loneliness is available to each of us, all the time. Not long ago I read about a power failure in a Salt Lake City hotel that left an elevator stuck between floors in total darkness—a frightening situation. Rescue workers, hearing a woman's voice inside, called out, "Are you alone in there?" "I'm by myself," came the calm reply, "but I'm not alone." People soon caught on that she meant God was with her, protecting her, as indeed He was.

You don't have to be trapped in an elevator to practice the presence of God. You can talk to Him anyplace, anytime, about anything, and He will listen and respond.

Jesus said, "I am with you always, even unto the end of the world" (Matthew 28:20).

Hold fast to that assurance, and the dark shadows of loneliness will fade away.

8
The Three Biggest Steps on the Road to Success

We sometimes talk as if imaging were a modern discovery, something that we in our twentieth-century wisdom have brought to light. Maybe in a way our generation *has* rediscovered imaging, but actually it is older than the Pyramids. Much older.

The other night, for example, I was reading an article about the marvelous cave paintings of southern France and northern Spain that are said to be at least twenty-five thousand years old. In those paintings, figures of men armed with spears are shown attacking animals resembling buffalo or bison. The article said that the drawings were part of primitive rituals designed to bring these cave-dwelling hunters good luck in their ceaseless quest for food.

In other words, before the dawn of history men were vividly imaging goals essential to their survival and reinforcing those images by painting them with primitive but lasting colors on the ceilings or walls of the caves that were their homes.

Now, hundreds of centuries later, we don't go forth with sharpened sticks or flint-tipped spears to hunt woolly mammoths or ward off saber-toothed tigers. But modern man still has to make a living in a tough, competitive, sometimes hostile world. The twentieth-century salesman who stalks his customer through the concrete canyons of a modern city is not very different from his remote ancestor in his primary goal, which is to put food on the table for his family. And just as the caveman tried to reinforce the image of himself as a successful hunter, so the modern breadwinner must reinforce and believe in his ability to wrest a living from the world that surrounds him.

I'm convinced that successful people in all walks of life use imaging constantly, whether they know it or not. So in this chapter let us talk a bit about the part it plays in pursuing that often elusive will-o'-the-wisp called success.

Imaging can help in three crucial areas. The first is goal setting. If any endeavor is to succeed, the first thing you must do is choose your goal, visualize it clearly, and fix a specific date for arriving at it.

Several years ago a young man came to me and announced rather forcefully that he wanted to "get somewhere" in life. He seemed to think that I could help him on his way. "I want to make something of myself," he announced. He pounded his fist into his hand. "Yes, sir, I'm determined to get somewhere."

"That's fine," I said to him. "Where do you want to get?"

"I don't know exactly," he told me, a bit taken aback. "I just want to achieve something worthwhile."

"Well," I said, "when do you want to achieve this ambition?"

"Oh, sooner or later," he said. "The sooner the better."

I tried again. "Tell me," I said, "what, exactly, do you want to do with yourself?"

He gave me a rather injured look. "If I knew that," he said, "I wouldn't be here bothering you."

"Look," I said to him, "you must have certain areas of interest or aptitude. What sort of thing appeals to you, or comes naturally to you? If you could wave a wand and have a career happen to you, what would it be?"

He shook his head sadly. "Those are tough questions. I really don't have the answers."

"Let me be blunt," I said. "You say you want to get somewhere. Well, you'll never get anywhere unless you know where that somewhere is. You have to have a special goal firmly fixed in your mind, a goal that you can see as plainly as you see me sitting in front of you right now. Not only that, you need to have a target date for achieving that goal. Not a vague point somewhere in the future. An actual date. A deadline. And once you've set a deadline, you must image yourself meeting it precisely on the nose. Do you understand what I'm saying to you?"

Somewhat hesitantly he said that he did.

Write Your Goal

"Now, I suggest that you go home and write down what you want to do with your life. Until you write a goal, it is only a wish; written, it becomes a focused objective. Put it down on paper. When it is on paper, boil it down to a single sentence: what you want to do, exactly when you intend to start (which should be right now), exactly when you plan to achieve your goal. Nothing fuzzy or hazy. Everything sharp and clear and definite. No reservations or qualifications. Just one strong, simple, declarative sentence. Then send me a copy of that life-changing sentence, because that is what it is going to do: change your life!"

"My life?" he echoed.

"Exactly," I told him. "Change you from a fumbling, bumbling, confused drifter and dreamer into a confident, focused, productive, useful person. I want you to make half a dozen copies of that sentence and put them where you'll see them at least three times a day. I want that pledge to sink down through all the levels of your conscious mind and deep into your unconscious mind, because that is where it will unlock the energies that you will need to achieve your goal. You will be imaging with power."

He shook his head slowly. "How can you be so sure of all this?" he demanded. "How do you know?"

"I know," I told him, "because when I was about your age, my father made me do just what I'm urging you to do. I was hesitating between two careers, one in journalism, one in the ministry. My father made me think it through and write down my chief goal in life in one sentence. That sentence was: 'Serve the Lord Jesus Christ and spread His Word as far as I possibly can in the course of my lifetime.'

"When I showed my father that sentence, he said, 'All right; that's it. Now if you will print those words on your conscious and subconscious mind, pray without ceasing, and work like the devil, that goal will come to pass.' So that is what I've tried to do. That is what I'm still trying to do with every ounce of strength and energy in me."

My visitor was silent for a while. Finally he said, "All right. I'll go home and do it." And he did. He sent me a copy of the sentence he finally wrote down. It is a large and praiseworthy and difficult objective, but if he does what my father said, if he will print it on his mind, image it, pray about it, and "work like the devil," I know he will achieve it. He has already made significant progress in the imaged direction.

Imaging a goal is a kind of promissory note made out to yourself. And even when these pledges are made casually, or only half-seriously, the unconscious mind can hear them and react to them. I have a novelist friend who told me that when he was a cub reporter on a small newspaper, not much more than a messenger boy, really, his father grew impatient with his apparent lack of progress and wrote him a letter asking him if he thought he would ever amount to anything in his chosen profession.

"I was a little annoyed at his lack of confidence in me," my friend said, "so I sat down and wrote him a note, half-joking and half-serious. I admitted that I seemed to be making little progress, but I added that I was only twenty-one and had a lot of time stretching out before me. Furthermore, I told my father, I knew exactly where I was going and when I would arrive. I said that at age thirty I would be a great newspaper reporter. At forty a great city editor. At fifty a great short-story writer. At sixty a great novelist. At seventy a great grandfather. At eighty a great admirer of pretty women. And at ninety a great loss to the community."

My friend went on to say that his father was much amused. "But you know," he added, "leaving aside the question of greatness or lack of it, my career has followed that predicted pattery to a remarkable degree."

"Of course it has," I told him. "You had a realizable wish, a realizable dream, a realizable image. You pointed the compass of your subconscious mind in the direction of that dream. And that is where it has carried you."

You'll notice that my novelist friend almost instinctively set time limits for each successive stage of his development. "By my thirtieth birthday," he said to himself, "I will be this; by my fortieth I'll be that; by my fifieth I will have achieved this set of goals," and so on. And his unconscious mind took him quite literally. It will always be obedient to a strong, definite self-image.

This deadline technique is extremely important in major ambitions and in minor ones. A woman approached me one night after I had given a talk in a West Coast city. She had quite a lovely face, but it was supported by a truly massive body. She looked almost as wide as she was high. She said abruptly, "How old do you think I am?" Then, when I hemmed and hawed a bit, she said, "Come on. No evasions. Tell me the truth. How old do you think I am?"

"Well," I said, "I'm no expert in these matters. But I'd say you are forty-eight or forty-nine." (And maybe I was stretching the truth a bit at that.)

She said, "I am thirty-five! Isn't it awful? I'm so fat it is a disgrace. I hate being like this. Every day I look in the mirror and see myself not as an attractive woman, which I used to be, but as an obese female. Have you ever heard a more disgusting description than this?"

"Yes, obese male," I interjected.

"Well," she continued, "I look into the future and see myself getting even heavier and even more unattractive. And I get so discouraged and depressed that life doesn't seem worth living. Can you help me?"

"Well," I said, "perhaps I can help you help yourself.

But first we are going to have to change the image you have of yourself, especially when you look into the future."

She Images Her Weight Goal

I found a place where we could talk without interruption, and made her sit down. "Now," I said, "tell me how much you weigh right this moment."

"One hundred eighty-seven pounds," she said sorrowfully.

"And how much do you want to weigh?"

"A lot less than this," she said.

"No," I insisted. "Give me an exact number of pounds."

"All right," she said. "I want to weigh one hundred twenty-eight pounds."

"And what do you want your measurements to be?"

She looked at me as if this were a strange question to be coming from a minister. "I haven't thought about that," she said.

I took a pencil and on the back of an envelope drew a simple outline of a human figure. "Here," I said. "Take this drawing. Add arrows pointing to waist, hips, bust. Put numerals alongside the arrows indicating the number of inches you want to measure in each area."

She took the pencil and wrote down some numbers.

"Good," I said. "Memorize those numbers. Tell your body that is the size it is going to be. Now, when do you want to be this size and weight? Next week?"

She smiled. "I know it won't happen overnight."

"Ah," I said, "but that means you can conceive of its happening, which wasn't the case a few minutes ago. Now, let us pick a target date. How about the first of January? That is eleven months away. If you want to lose fifty-nine pounds, that is only a fraction over five pounds a month—less than two pounds a week. That certainly is obtainable. And if you believe you can, you will do it. You have to visualize the pounds melting away. You have to see yourself fitting into smaller dresses. You have to anticipate the admiration on your husband's face as the girl he married emerges from the prison she has been living in.

"Finally, you have to look into the mirror and image, not an obese female, but a new and vibrant and beautiful woman who has a rendezvous with next New Year's Day. If you hold that image in your mind for one minute every morning when you wake up and one minute every night just before you fall asleep, and if you ask God for spiritual strength to persevere, the dream will actualize itself. I'm sure of it. And I want you to send me a telegram next January first, telling me that I was right."

Well, the telegram didn't come, and I was a bit disappointed. But about a week later, when I was shaking hands with members of the congregation after Sunday service at Marble Collegiate Church, a beautiful, slender woman shook my hand and asked, "How old am I?" I stared at her in amazement. "Oh, it's you!" I exclaimed, because at first I hadn't recognized her as the "obese female" from out west. But here she was, completely transformed. I asked, "One hundred twenty-eight pounds?" She said, "One hundred twenty-seven and a half! Thanks to you!"

"Don't thank me," I said. "Thank the good Lord for working with you all these months. And in particular, thank Him for the power that He put into your unconscious mind through imaging, the power that turns wishes into realities when the wishes are strong enough."

If setting worthy goals is the first step on the road to success, the second is the belief—no, the conviction—that you are capable of achieving those goals. There has to be in your mind the unshakable image of yourself *succeeding* at the goal you have set yourself. The more vivid this image is, the more obtainable the goal becomes.

Great athletes have always known this. The high jumper "sees" himself skimming over the bar; the golfer facing a difficult shot images the ball soaring over the intervening obstacles and landing squarely on the green; the placekicker in football keeps his head down as he kicks, but in his mind's eye he holds the mental picture of what he wants to happen in the next few seconds. He "sees" the great arena full of tense spectators, the onrushing defensive linemen, the blockers holding them off, the ball spiraling back to the holder, the thud as his foot connects with it at precisely the right angle, then its spinning flight squarely between the uprights. The more intensely he images this before it happens, the higher his confidence in himself and the better his chances of making it happen.

Discard the Failure Image

Even people who have a long record of *not* succeeding can be turned into tremendous achievers if they will discard their images of themselves as failures or ne'er-do-wells and become God-trusting individuals whose attainment of desired goals is just a matter of time, and a specific length of time at that.

In Australia a few years ago, I met a remarkable man named John "Bert" Walton. He has since become a close friend. He told me that when he started out in life he seemed to be caught in a peculiar failure pattern. Whatever he tried would start out well and then end up badly. As a schoolboy he dropped out of several schools for this reason. He became convinced that it was his destiny in life to make good beginnings and then watch them fade away. And naturally, since that was how he saw or imaged himself, that was what always happened.

At one point, he got a job with the Australian division of a famous American company. The same dreary pattern seemed to be unfolding: He started out well and then things began to slide. This didn't surprise him much; it was what he expected to happen.

Then the company sent a motivational speaker out to give some talks to their Australian employees, and Bert Walton was in the audience. The visitor told his listeners that they could achieve anything they wanted to, if they would just believe that they could do it. He told them to visualize themselves moving up in the company, receiving promotions, gaining energy and dynamism as they went, right up to the very top. "You can if you think you can," he kept saying. "Most of you are only using ten percent of the powers that are in you. Most of you are letting the fear of failure hold you back. Most of you are living in a dungeon of self-depreciation and negative thinking. All the ingredients of success are right there inside you, if you'll just turn your thinking around. Don't keep telling yourself you can't do this or you can't do that. Knock the *T* off the word *can't*. You can do anything—ANYTHING—if you think you can!"

Bert Walton had never heard anything like this in his whole life. He told me that he walked away from the lecture almost in a state of shock. He realized for the first time that his image of himself as a person who started well and then faded away was all in his head, a state of mind that could be altered any time he made a firm decision to alter it. He said, "I walked past the office of the head of operations for New South Wales, and I visualized myself in that job. I imaged myself sitting at that desk. I said to myself, 'I can have that job if I think I can have it, and from now on I do think I can. I know I can. I'm going to have it. I *will* have it. And then I'll move on from there!'"

Bert Walton went back to work with tremendous enthusiasm and confidence and energy. He received promotions. He became manager of operations for New South Wales. Finally he became the head of the company for all of Australia. I was told by other Australian friends of mine that he probably could have become the head of the parent company also, but his career took another turn. His father was the owner of a store and wanted his son to come in with him. So Bert Walton built that store into one of the largest merchandising chains in Australia. He was knighted by the queen. Where once he had been dogged by failure, now everything he did was crowned by success. "I'm not an unusual person," he told me. "I really have only an ordinary brain. It was that one talk that changed my self-image by giving it a little twist. It made me see myself differently, and so I was different."

"Well," I told him, "if you have only an ordinary mind, you have certainly used it in an extraordinary manner!" And indeed he has. Sir John Walton is a living example of imaging, of positive thinking and faith.

People who want to succeed in life not only have to build a strong self-image but they also have to get that image across to the people whose goodwill and support they need to get ahead. All successful salesmen know this. When I was a youngster growing up in Bellefontaine, Ohio, there were only two Jewish families in town. One was in the clothing business. Emil Geiger ran the leading men's clothing store. Emil was a good friend of my father—he used to come to our church to hear my father preach because there was no synagogue in town. Everybody liked Emil. If a customer came in and Emil couldn't fit him or supply him with what he needed, Emil would courteously direct him to another store that could. "I'm not just selling clothes," he used to say. "I'm selling the reputation of Emil Geiger as someone who wants to help his fellowman. The secret of success in business is this: Think of the customer's needs, not your own. Create the image of yourself as someone who cares about the customer, not about the customer's money, and you will always do well."

Emil used to give me odd jobs now and then. I remember that one time he had a lot of old marked-down suits that nobody wanted to buy, so he persuaded me to take a friend of mine and go out into the countryside with a horse and wagon and try to sell the suits to farmers. "Tell them these suits are good merchandise even though they are marked down. And the suits will serve them well. Be sure that each customer is happy with his purchase." Emil was pleased with our successful sales campaign.

Years later, Emil came to New York and heard me preach. Afterward, in my study, he said, "Well, Norman, you've come a long way from Bellefontaine, but you are still a salesman, just as I trained you to be. You are offering something that people want and you are thinking about their needs, not your own. What's more, you see yourself as a successful seller of ideas, and so other people accept that image of you, too, and listen to what you have to say. If you just keep on giving people what they know they need, and make them feel you care about them, they will come from miles around to hear you." I shall always cherish

Emil's memory, for he cared enough to help me when I was a boy.

Another friend of mine who projects his own self-image into the minds of his customers is Joe Girard, listed in the *Guinness Book of World Records* as the world's greatest automobile salesman. There was a time in Joe Girard's life when he looked like the world's greatest failure. Everything he touched went wrong. He was up to his ears in debt. The bank was trying to repossess his house, his car, everything.

One cold night in January he came home, climbing the back fence and sneaking in the back door to avoid bill collectors. When he walked into the kitchen, his wife told him that there was no food in the house. She had nothing to give the children. At that moment the doorbell rang. Another bill collector.

Joe Girard didn't open the front door. Instead, he stooped down in the darkened hallway and prayed a prayer of desperation. He was convinced that he was a total failure as a husband, as a provider, as a human being. He asked the Lord to help him, to give him another image of himself, to turn his life around.

The next day he went to an automobile-sales agency where he knew the manager, and begged him for a selling job. The man felt sorry for him and agreed to give him a chance on a commission basis. All that day he dialed people he knew, trying to sell a car by phone, but nothing happened. The timing was unfortunate, just after the Christmas season. It seemed nobody was buying cars.

Making a Sale Gets Him Started

Finally, just before closing time, a man wandered in. Just looking, he said. He had no intention of buying anything. By now, Joe Girard should have been totally discouraged. But somehow, looking at the man, he visualized a warm, friendly encounter that would result in a sale. He imaged himself receiving the commission money, then bringing home bags of groceries to his family. He saw the food steaming on the table, the hungry children enjoying it. He fixed the whole scene in his mind; then he began to talk in a friendly and outgoing spirit to the man, whom he now saw as a promising prospect. In the end, impressed by Joe's sincerity, the man agreed to buy a car. The owner of the agency gave Joe an advance on his commission that enabled him to go out and buy those groceries. He took them home. The whole dream came true.

After that, there was no stopping Joe as a salesman. He never let his customers forget who he was or what he did for a living. He kept records and sent each customer a card on his or her birthday. If they were Irish, he sent them a card on Saint Patrick's Day. If they were Jewish, he sent them one on Jewish holidays. With each sale, his image of himself as the most effective car salesman in the world grew stronger. And he continues to put that image into the thinking of prospective customers to this day.

If the first step on the road to success is to set a goal, and the second is to believe you can reach it, and the third is to image it, the fourth and most important is this: Let God be your partner. God stands ready to help you at all times. I know this, for He has always helped me. And that is for sure. He gives quiet but accurate guidance to those who ask for it. He gives determination to the hesitant, and courage to the fainthearted.

The combination of strong imaging backed by strong faith is irresistible. Years ago, a young woman named Blanche Green, who had always led a sheltered life, married a schoolteacher. Five years later her husband had a serious accident that left him an invalid. It was a frightening situation for the young woman.

But Blanche was a deeply religious woman. She was a believer in God and so in herself. As she prayed for help and guidance, an image came to her. It seemed to involve a company that dealt in women's clothing, and she also seemed to see herself playing an important part in the company. This puzzled her because she had no connection with the clothing industry.

Then she happened to meet two young men who were in the clothing business. The wife of one had designed a new kind of foundation garment for women. The men had the patent for it, but no money with which to launch it. It was still in the idea stage, going nowhere.

But to Blanche this chance meeting was a clear directive from the Lord; she saw it as divine guidance. She told the two young men that she was sure she could sell their new design profitably for them.

Naturally they asked her what selling experience she had had.

"None," she told them. "But I know how it should be done. You get the name of a prospect. Then you pray for that prospect. Then you believe that a helpful and friendly meeting will take place with that prospect. You form a picture in your mind of a successful encounter. You believe that God is always with you. You go out in the name of the Lord, and you meet that prospect, and you sell her the garment."

"Oh, you're crazy!" they said.

"No," she said, "I'm not crazy. If you go out in the name of the Lord, being loving and honest and caring, holding the success picture, the doors will open for you. If you let me try it, you will see."

Reluctantly, they let her try. So this pretty young woman, with no business experience at all but with a positive attitude, went out every day selling door-to-door. As she approached each door, she would affirm to herself, "If God be for me, who [or what] can be against me?" Her manner was so calm and so friendly and so open that people trusted her instinctively. "I'm going to help American women shape up," she used to tell her customers, smiling. And she did. In the end she became the president of a successful corset company and a legend in the garment industry.

The reason for Blanche Green's success was as simple as it was powerful. Faith in God removes tension, fear, worry, and all the negative forces that hold a person back from success. If God be for you (and if your goal is a worthy one, He *will* be for you), then what is there to worry about? If the most powerful force in the universe is on your side, why should you have any fear of failure? A kind of serenity comes over people who have this conviction, and in the center of that serenity more often than not is the sunlit oasis that we call success.

Serenity. That is a most important contribution of religion, isn't it? Religion is a set of beliefs and attitudes that gives calmness and assurance to struggling human beings, gives them the courage and determination they need to get through this life, plus a blueprint that, if followed, will lead them triumphantly into the life to come.

I see this serenity at work in God-trusting people all the time. Not long ago I was in the office of a well-known industrialist, a self-made man in the automotive industry. It was late afternoon, quitting time. I knew he had a tremendously heavy schedule, but his desk was completely clear, not a single piece of unfinished business on it. I complimented him on that. "How do you do it?" I asked him.

"Well," he said, "there was a time when I would finish up a day with papers all over my desk, each one representing an unsolved problem. I tried to figure out what was wrong, and finally I came to the conclusion that I was worrying too much. I hesitated to make decisions because I worried about whether they were the right decisions. I worried about the consequences of the decisions I did make. Worry was acting as a kind of paralysis, slowing me down, holding me back."

"Evidently you got rid of it," I said. "How did you manage that?"

"If you watch as we leave this office," he said, "I think you'll see."

When we did leave a few minutes later, I noticed on the wall near the door a calendar, the kind where each day is indicated on a page that can be torn off and discarded. Underneath the calendar was a scrap basket. My friend paused at the door, tore off the top sheet of the calendar, and slowly crumpled it into a ball. He closed his eyes and his lips moved soundlessly. Finally he opened his hand and let the crumpled piece of paper drop into the scrap basket.

"Great invention, the scrap basket," he said with a smile. "When you want to get rid of something, all you have to do is drop it there and it is gone. So that's what I do with my worries at the end of every day. I ask the Lord to watch over my responsibilities while I am away from this office. I thank Him for His love and His care. Then I open my hand and let the worries and the problems of the day simply disappear." He snapped his fingers. "Just like that! I know there will be new problems the next day, but I don't worry about them. The Lord will help me deal with them. And anyway, the energy I save by not worrying today will be channeled into problem solving tomorrow!

"I ask the Lord to watch over my responsibilities while I'm away from this office." That man had taken the fourth and crucial step on the road to success by asking God to be his partner in decision making. He asked for support and guidance. He *imaged* the infinite wisdom and sagacity of the Almighty being focused on his problems, untangling them, clarifying them, working out solutions that would appear, when the time was right, in flashes of insight or nudges of intuition in his own mind. He built his house upon the rock, knowing that when the sea of troubles swirled around it, it would still stand.

When you do that, you don't have to worry about pursuing success or happiness. They will come to you.

9
Imaging—Key to Health?

Near the end of World War II, a young American soldier named Lew Miller was caught in a burst of German machine-gun fire. Five bullets smashed into him: two in his left arm, one in his shoulder, two in his head. He was taken to a military hospital more dead than alive.

Weeks passed, then months. His normal weight of 192 pounds dropped to 90. He was so weak that if he tried to stand, he fell on his face. He was a brave man and he struggled valiantly to regain his strength, but recovery was so slow and painful that it seemed almost hopeless.

He tried praying, but his prayers seemed feeble and futile to him. Doctors did their best, but their best seemed to make little difference.

Sometimes, to make the endless hours pass more quickly, Lew Miller would try to recall happy scenes from the past, athletic triumphs he had had as a boy, or occasions when he had won scholastic prizes or honors. He would picture the applause of the crowds, the pride and happiness on his parents' faces, the satisfaction he had felt. He tried to visualize these events as vividly as possible, because when he did he could forget, momentarily, the hospital bed where he lay.

As he reviewed these memories, Lew Miller began to be aware that most of them seemed to have a common denominator. Each time he had scored a triumph or gained an objective, he had had a mental picture of the success before it actually happened. Whether it was winning a tennis tournament or placing in the first ten runners in a cross-country race, he had "seen" himself doing it in advance, and when he clung to that image with unswerving faith, the actuality seemed in some uncanny way to follow the dream.

Lew Miller had plenty of time to think, and gradually he began to see (just as years later Harry DeCamp would see) a connection between this before-and-after pattern and some of the great promises of the New Testament. He remembered that "what things soever ye desire, when ye pray, believe that ye receive them, and ye shall have them." Was it possible, Lew Miller asked himself, that a strong mental image, backed by intense faith, could actually be a form of silent prayer, prayer unencumbered by words? And if that were so, might he not hasten his own recovery by visualizing it happening and claiming Christ's promise at the same time?

Lew Miller had believed all along in the power of God, but now he began to see that to liberate that power in his own life it was *his* responsibility to create the image of his own recovery and nurture it with faith. And so, with a sudden surge of determination and energy, he began to do just that. He saw himself returning home. He saw himself driving a car, holding down a job, resuming a normal, everyday sort of life. Looking beyond that, he saw himself raising a family, taking part in civic affairs, pursuing a career. Not only did he visualize these things over and over, with all possible intensity, but he also began to thank God *in advance* for turning these visions into reality.

"We are essentially minds with bodies," Lew Miller told himself, "not the other way around. Therefore our minds can dominate and control our bodies. If I affirm and visualize my recovery, my thoughts will steadily be forming and producing their physical counterparts."

As soon as all these concepts came together in Lew Miller's mind, he felt a remarkable upsurge of hope and well-being. To the doctors' amazement, he began to mend rapidly. Today Lew Miller is a happily married man with two children. He leads the normal, happy, and productive life that he imaged so vividly in that army hospital so many years ago. He is convinced that he groped his way to one of the most powerful healing combinations in the world: intense imaging plus unshakable faith. And it brought him back from the edge of the grave to the land of the living.

What does medical science make of stories like this one? Naturally, there is division of opinion. Some doctors believe that all illness is a reflection of mental or emotional states. Others do not go that far. And certainly a layman like myself cannot pretend to be a judge.

I was interested to read a brochure announcing a course called "Guided Imagery and the Bodymind Approach to Optimum Health," by Jeanne Archterberg, Ph.D., and G. Frank Lawlis, Ph.D. This brochure, in describing the program to be offered, stated:

> Imagery has been the golden thread running through effective medical practice for over 3,000 years. Imagery appears to be the bridge between psyche and soma; it is central to learning biofeedback . . . and may be the basis for understanding and increasing the power of the placebo effect. As such, imagery may well prove to be the single most important technique for modern health care.

Thirty years ago an authority on psychosomatic medicine, Dr. Arnold A. Hutschnecker, wrote, "We, ourselves, choose the time of illness, the kind of illness, the course of illness, and its gravity." And he added, "We are moving toward a recognition that in illness of any kind, from the common cold to cancer, emotional stress plays a part."

Not long ago I came across a newspaper story in which a California physician, Dr. Irving Oyle, was quoted as saying that people could live to be 150 years old if they would just practice a combination of right thinking and prayer. "Positive, beautiful thoughts trigger the release of beneficial hormones in the body and these in turn help the body to heal itself." On the other hand, he said, "If you presume that you live in a hostile universe, the reaction to that presumption is what wears out your body." Then he added, "Prayer is a good way to combat anxiety and promote healing.... When you pray, you assume that there is some force in this universe which is on your side—some powerful force. The minute you do that, your body. relaxes. And if you really believe that God will respond to you, you have immediately instituted the healing process. Faith itself creates the hormones that make you live longer."

Basic Keys to Healing

Hope, faith, truth—these seem to be the keys. When you have them, you can image your own recovery and speed the healing process. When you don't have them, you can't. Dr. Sanford Cohen, Chief of Psychiatry at Boston University School of Medicine, has made some studies that seem to indicate that hopelessness—that is, an image of no recovery—actually kills. If a doctor diagnoses a fatal disease and tells the patient, and if the patient loses hope and gives up, death comes quickly. An autopsy may show the malignancy, all right, but no reason the patient should have died so soon.

I once knew a woman whose elderly father was hit by a taxi as he was crossing a street in Manhattan and died at the age of eighty-seven. When an autopsy was performed, the doctor was amazed. "Your father had all sorts of lesions and ailments that should have caused his death twenty years ago," he said to the woman. "Yet you say he was lively and energetic right up to the end. How do you account for that?"

"I don't know," the woman said, "unless it was his habit of saying to me every single morning, 'Today is going to be a terrific day.'" This daily imaging habit, it seems, paid off.

A doctor friend once showed me X rays of three human hearts. He said, "What do you think of those hearts?"

"Well," I said, "I know nothing about hearts or X rays. Is something wrong with them?"

The doctor said, "You are looking at three damaged hearts. The owners of these hearts were negative people; they all expected to get ill or be ill; two of them expected to die young. On top of that, all three were living irresponsibly. I guess you might say their lives were full of sin."

"Were you able to help them?" I asked.

"In part," he said. "I took over your job. I showed them, with these X rays, how the way they were living and the way they were thinking was affecting their hearts. I told them that if they went on much longer, their hearts would lose the capacity to rebound, but if they changed their attitudes and their habits and their thinking, their hearts could still recover because of the marvelous comeback potential the Creator had built into them." He chuckled. "I guess you could say I scared the hell [sin] out of them. Those people are healthy, vigorous, alive people today because they finally grasped the connection between their minds and their hearts, between moral or immoral living and the functioning of the most important organ in their bodies. You could make a sermon out of this, Norman. If you do, I suggest you tell your congregation that their bodies will take a lot of abuse, but the point finally comes where it won't take anymore— and people had better turn away from downbeat thinking and wrong living before that point is reached, because afterward it is too late."

Ruth and I have lived quite a few years now, and both of us have been remarkably free of illness all along the way. Ruth attributes her good health partly to the fact that as a child she ate simple foods, mostly vegetables. Money was scarce in the Stafford family, so there was seldom any meat. Ruth says she never tasted steak or rare roast beef until she went to college. She also thinks there is a strong connection between hard work and good health. "If you keep really busy," she says—and she certainly does—"you don't have time to think about yourself or your health. Or your lack of health."

As for me, I'm convinced that human beings are *sup-*

posed to be healthy; we are *designed* to be healthy; that is what the Creator intended when He made us. I constantly image myself as a disease-free individual. It reminds me of something an airline pilot told me one day when he came back through the plane to visit with us passengers. I said to him, "It always amazes me how these big planes stay up in the air. All this tremendous weight, all this fuel, all of these people, all their baggage. It is astonishing!"

"Not really," the pilot said. "It is the nature of airplanes to stay up in the air. They are designed to fly. The want to stay up in the air. It is very hard for a plane *not* to stay up in the air, because that is the way they are put together."

That is the way God put us together, too. To be healthy, energetic, creative, dynamic people at every age, full of vitality and health. I'm sure of it.

But we have a responsibility, too, not to abuse our bodies with alcohol or drugs or nicotine or other harmful substances, or too much food, for that matter. Nor should we abuse ourselves with overtension. It is hard to persuade people to avoid these things, especially young people, because they have great vitality and think they are immune to trouble and can go on indefinitely. They have to learn the hard way, and that can be unpleasant.

The other night I was reading a book by my friend Art Linkletter, the TV personality. Art doesn't touch tobacco, and in the book he told why. When he was still just a youngster he got a job as a welder. A lot of the older welders chewed tobacco or dipped snuff and—wanting to be one of the boys—young Art was ready to try either or both.

But one of the welders, a big, tough fellow, said, "Let me show you something, son. Take off your shoe and sock." When Art did, the man stuck a big wad of tobacco between two of Art's toes. "Now put your shoe and sock back on," he said, "and see what happens."

Within a short time, Art began to feel ill. Before long he was desperately nauseated. The chemicals in the tobacco had invaded his whole system through the skin between his toes. And Art wrote: "At that moment I decided I was never going to smoke." And he never has.

That was pure chemical cause and effect. The interaction of mind and body is more subtle, but it is just as real. And the interaction of infinite mind, which is God, and the human organism, across the bridge known as prayer, is more mysterious still. But every minister and most laymen have seen unforgettable examples of it.

I remember one night when I was a young minister in Syracuse, New York, a telephone call came from a physician I knew, Dr. Gordon Hoople. He said he had a patient who was not responding to treatment. A crisis was imminent. He wanted me to come right away.

When I arrived at the home, I found Dr. Hoople and a young nurse with the patient, a middle-aged woman who seemed to be in a coma. I recognized the nurse as a member of my own congregation.

"This woman is very ill," the doctor said. "I've done everything I can for her medically, but that is not enough. I treat my patients, but it is God who does the healing. You know that and I know it. Now here we are, three believers and this woman, who is unconscious. Let us try to fill this room with the healing grace of the greatest of all physicians, Jesus Christ. Let us image her as responding to the creative life-force. Actually there is no medical reason that she should die. But her spirit seems weak. Let's put faith into that spirit."

Scripture Reaches Into Unconscious

I remember we sat down by the bedside. First I prayed. Then Hoople prayed. Then the young nurse prayed. Then we began to quote Scripture passages. It was a strange and moving experience. I felt as if there were two contending forces in the room, one regenerative, the other destructive, and that by praying and affirming faith through Scripture, we were adding strength to the life-force. I found that I could summon to mind almost any Bible passage I wanted and could recite it verbatim, even though ordinarily I could not have done this. Later, Hoople and the nurse told me they had the same experience.

Hours passed. Nothing changed. Then, all at once, the patient opened her eyes, smiled at us faintly, and fell into a quiet sleep. I remember how Hoople reached out and felt her pulse with his sensitive fingers. "It's all right now," he said. "The crisis is over. Our prayers and our affirmative faith have pulled her through." And she did indeed get well.

A less dramatic incident, but one which I remember vividly, happened some years ago when I was driving from Dayton, Ohio, to the little village of Bowersville, where I was born. The town was celebrating its one hundredth anniversary, and I had been invited, as a native son, to give the centennial address.

As I drove along, my ear began to ache. I hadn't had an earache since childhood, but now I had one that grew worse and worse. By the time we reached Bowersville, I was in agony. I asked Ruth to go into the hall where I was scheduled to give my talk and tell the people in charge that I was indisposed, that they would have to delay the talk, that perhaps I couldn't deliver it at all.

When Ruth was gone, I sat holding my head in my hands, hardly able to believe the amount of pain that could be generated by one misbehaving ear. As I sat there, I heard a tap on the window of the car and a stranger spoke to me. I remember he was a big man with a calm, kindly face. He evidently knew who I was, for he spoke my name. "You're not well?" he asked. I assured him that I was far from well. "I'm a believer," he said, "and I have the gift of healing. I'd like to give you a faith treatment. I think it might help."

I was suspicious. "What does it consist of?" I wanted to know.

"I'll put my hands on your ears," he said, "and offer a prayer of healing. I'll tell the Lord that you are needed here tonight. It is the town's birthday and people are waiting to hear you. I'll ask Him to take away the pain."

"What do I have to do?" I asked.

"Just believe," he said, "and picture yourself as healed of this pain that is tormenting you."

So I agreed. While he prayed, with his hands covering

my ears, I tried to hold in mind an image of myself with two good, healthy, nonaching ears. And, to my astonishment, almost instantly the pain began to subside. It didn't vanish in one split second, but it began to diminish steadily. The man had told me to believe and visualize and I had tried, but the relief was so remarkable that I could hardly believe it. I tried to thank the man, but he simply smiled and moved away.

A moment later, Ruth came back. She had found a medical doctor and had him with her. I told him what had happened. By now the pain was perhaps 60 percent gone.

"Well," said the doctor, "that's fine, but I would like to give you a shot of antibiotic anyway."

So, at Ruth's urging, I let him give me the shot, and I'm sure it had good effect, also. Anyway, the pain continued to subside, and soon after that I was able to give my talk with almost no discomfort. Who healed me? Was it the faith healer or the doctor? Both, perhaps, plus the power of the creative image. However it may be explained, I have had no further earaches to this very day.

How can we explain the spiritual power when it is called upon that way? We can't explain it, but we know it is there. We know it works. When a prayer chain is organized for someone who is sick, with dozens or perhaps hundreds of people praying for the same result, that collective imaging of the patient's improvement can release enormous curative powers. I have seen it happen over and over again.

Belief in the power of prayer and in spiritual procedures should in no way diminish our respect and gratitude for medical science. Both are gifts from God and both, in my opinion, should be used to the utmost when needed. But science has limits. However, the power of prayer is limitless to the degree that it enables us to make contact with God, who made our bodies. I remember how my old friend Dr. Smiley Blanton handled one difficult psychiatric case. The doctor tried every possible medical approach. Nothing worked. Finally the famous psychiatrist, then an older doctor, handed the man a Bible. "Here," he said. "Take this. Go away and read it. Then just do whatever Jesus says. See yourself as a well, normal, healthy person. If you just do that, you'll be all right."

How I Stopped Having Colds

Holding a strong mental image of yourself as a healthy person definitely reduces your susceptibility to illness. I used to have the annoying habit of getting a bad cold every February. (I tried not to get it on a Sunday, because that would have interfered with my preaching.) It always went through the same cycle: sniffling, achiness, sore throat, then the vocal cords would close up and all I could do was croak unintelligibly. Finally, about four years ago, I said to myself, "This is ridiculous. It is all in your head. You expect to get a cold when February comes. You image it and so you get one. Now put that image out of your mind. Forget it. Instead, image yourself *not* having a cold in February and see what happens." So I did—and I haven't had a cold since. Ruth says dryly that she began making me take more vitamins at about that time, and perhaps she did. But I think the changed image in my mind was the main thing.

I remember one unusual case where negative images were put to a positive use. The man involved was prominent in literary and publishing circles in New York. He was very successful professionally, but he was an alcoholic. Sober, he was brilliant and charming, but drunk he was an obnoxious boor who embarrassed his friends, humiliated his wife, wrecked his automobiles, and in general was very bad news indeed.

This man would go without drinking for weeks, sometimes months. Then he would convince himself that the problem was licked, that he could handle a drink or two. But he never could. Once he took the first drink, he couldn't stop. He would drink until he passed out, sometimes in a bar, sometimes in the street, usually after creating some dismal scene.

When he came to himself after these binges, he was always filled with remorse, self-loathing, and disgust. He would vow never to touch another drop of alcohol. But then, as the memory faded, he would take the first fatal step and go through the whole sordid cycle again. Nothing seemed to break the pattern. He tried Alcoholics Anonymous, but even that powerful rescue system could not help him.

One morning he woke up in Bellevue Hospital after another binge. He was sick, trembling, miserable, filled with guilt and self-condemnation. All around him were the sights and sounds and smells of a hospital ward filled with human wreckage of every description. *I'm in hell*, he thought, *and I put myself here. If I could just remember exactly how I'm feeling now, how ashamed I am, how utterly horrible all this is, I would never take another drink.*

If I could just remember. . . . After he was released and entered into another period of sobriety, he kept hearing echoes of that phrase, and the thought came to him that if once a day he would just image himself in the alcoholic ward, recall every sordid aspect of it, and relive every gruesome detail, the revulsion would be so strong that he would not take a drink that day.

So he decided that every day when the *idea* of alcohol presented itself to him for the first time—a whiskey advertisement in the morning paper, a beer commercial on the radio, the casual mention of a cocktail party, anything— he would stop whatever he was doing for one full minute and image, as vividly as possible, the horrors he had undergone (and put others through) each time he took that first drink.

He made this ironclad rule for himself, and he stuck to it rigidly. Even if he was having a telephone conversation and the subject of alcohol was mentioned, he would excuse himself, promise to call back, and then for one full minute picture himself back in the alcoholic ward—sick, miserable, remorseful, and ashamed.

And it worked. He never took another drink—a remarkable example of the positive power that can emerge from a negative image.

I believe the greatest health insurance a person can carry is to see himself, proudly and humbly, as a creation of God. God, who is infinitely gifted and infinitely wise, does not do bad work. If He created you in His image, and He did, that means that His perfection, His excellence, His craftsmanship are built into you. It follows then, does it not, that the best way to keep His handiwork in good running order is to stay close to Him.

The other day in a town where I had made a speech, a man filled with high spirits, zest, and goodwill greeted me with, "I still have the faucet."

I was baffled. "What do you mean, faucet?"

"Oh," he said, "don't you remember? You gave me the faucet idea." He went on to remind me of a talk I had given some twenty years ago, and presently I remembered the illustration he was referring to. At the time, I had been reading T. E. Lawrence's book *The Seven Pillars of Wisdom*. Lawrence was the great desert fighter of World War I who identified himself with the Arabs and became one of their leaders in their revolt against the Turks.

After the war, Lawrence took a few of his Arab friends from the burning sands of the desert to the boulevards of Paris. He put them up in one of the most elegant hotels. He showed them all the sights: the Champs Élysées, the Eiffel Tower, the tomb of Napoleon. But they were only mildly interested in these things. The one object in Paris that fascinated them was the faucet in the bathtub in their hotel. Lawrence would find them gathered around the tub turning on the faucet with exclamations of delight, and watching the strong stream of water which they could control at will. They kept saying, "Isn't this marvelous? All you do is turn a little wheel and you get all the water you want!" It was amazing to men who had lived all their lives on the hot and arid desert sands.

"You foolish fellows," Lawrence said to them. "Don't you know that this faucet is attached to a pipe, which leads to a network of pipes, which lead to great conduits, which lead to vast reservoirs? And don't you know that those reservoirs are so located that the melting snows and the rains from the mountains come surging into them? You cannot get water from a faucet unless it is connected to a source of water."

So the man who had heard me tell this story said, "That

little parable got through to me somehow. I realized that I badly needed a faucet attached to the vast reservoirs of God's power. I decided to go with Jesus Christ as the directing force in my life." He went on to say that he had stopped doing some things he had been doing, and where, before there had been no flow of power in his life, now it came surging through and had been flowing ever since.

So if your health isn't what it should be, if your life isn't what you want it to be, if you have not reached the level of attainment that you desire, then you can do what so many happy, successful people have done: get yourself attached to the flow of spiritual power. You can attach yourself to this incredible power by wanting to be attached; you can attach yourself by believing, by imaging, and by following the Word.

Then, once you are attached, you will live with the power coursing through you. This power is no fantasy. It is reality, absolute reality, and one of incredible strength. It can and does enter into believing persons and thereby into situations in a way so astonishing that it should convince anyone, however skeptical, that imaging the power of God can affect persons, even situations, under the most difficult circumstances.

Miracle of Imaging in New Zealand

For example, I received a letter from a man in Auckland, New Zealand, stating that he has written a book and asking permission to use certain quotations from our writings. Of his own book he said, "I have tried to make it a practical guide to a healthy self-image, as well as finding fulfillment in life through the use of a Master Picture Plan." The book is titled *The Greatest Sale You'll Ever Make—and How to Make It*. But this author points out that "while it [his book] is primarily designed for salesmen, the same techniques can be used by anybody."

But it was the P.S. to his letter that gave testimony to the amazing power of imaging faith. The P.S. reads:

I have been blind, but now through the power of Jesus, together with the inspiration provided by you, and the skill of a surgeon, I have got back sight in the left eye. When the local doctors said nothing could be done, I refused to accept it, telling them, "There must be someone, somewhere in the world who can help." In a wonderful way I was guided to a specialist in Melbourne, Australia, and had pioneer operations in Royal Melbourne Hospital. I took your booklet, "*You Can Overcome Any Problem*," with me, and used to finger it day and night. I was sent home, heavily drugged, and for two years was not allowed to work and then only for short periods.

The day came when I could slowly read the title *You— Can—Overcome—Any—Problem*, but the rest was blank. I kept on praying and holding your booklet and the day came when I could read your name. Finally, praise God, the time came when I could read what is inside. The piece I want permission to quote on P. 17, "So never let any problem overawe you . . ." to me is one of the greatest passages in the booklet. In the NAME OF CHRIST I refuse to be intimidated. Thank you Dr. Peale, thank you.

Bruce G. Hardie

The message is indeed impressive: "In the Name of Christ I refuse to be intimidated." Image the power, the wonder-working power, as healing, restoring. What you can image, you truly can be.

(If you would like a free copy of the booklet, "You Can Overcome Any Problem" referred to by Mr. Hardie, you may have it by writing to the Foundation for Christian Living, Pawling, New York, 12564.)

Actually, the creative healing effect of such mental attitudes and practices as positive thinking, faith, prayer, and imaging are underscored if not verified by the point of view of scientists.

In an article in the *Reader's Digest* for September 1980, Laurence Cherry describes the work of Dr. Lewis Thomas, president of the famed Memorial Sloan-Kettering Cancer Center in New York City, whom he quotes as saying: "The natural tendency of the human body is toward health—we are amazingly tough and durable." Dr. Thomas, it seems, takes an optimistic view of the basic health of the individual. "I believe fervently in our species and have no patience with the current fashion of running the human being down. On the contrary we are a spectacular, splendid manifestation of life. We matter. We are the newest, youngest, brightest thing around." So says Dr. Thomas in his book *The Medusa and the Snail*.

Dr. Thomas is of the opinion that most germs are either friendly, like the ones in our body that help digestion, or simply not interested in us. The few germs that do attack us are usually soon annihilated by the body's white blood cells.

"As for diseases whose care is unknown at the present time, Dr. Thomas believes that science will soon learn how to eradicate them," says Laurence Cherry, adding that "in the not very distant future Dr. Thomas predicts we will be able to live out our life span without worrying about illness. Many of the disablements considered an inevitable part of age are actually the result of a disease process, probably involving viruses. There is no reason why these, too, shouldn't ultimately be eliminated," he says.

Since the most creative element in our person, the superior factor in our entire entity, is the mind, such scientific findings as those of Dr. Lewis Thomas and other outstanding thinkers would certainly seem to support the thesis that mental activity, imaging or picturing health is a valid and productive process. It validates the affirmative belief that what you image you can be.

So visualize and picturize your own well-being. See yourself whole, healthy, and energized. Practice creative imaging—the key to health.

10
The Word That Undermines Marriage

We Americans should be good at imaging because we are an optimistic people. We think mistakes can be corrected. We believe obstacles can be overcome. We like to dream big—and what is dreaming, when it is focused intensely, but a powerful form of imaging?

It has always been this way in this country. The great nineteenth-century explorer, John C. Frémont, wrote of nights spent beside a flickering campfire on the great plains, listening to the coyotes howl and dreaming of mighty cities that someday would stand in the vast emptiness around him. Frémont's dreams must have seemed like the wildest fantasies at the time. But today, there the cities stand.

One of our most beloved patriotic songs, *America the Beautiful*, reflects this soaring optimism:

> O beautiful for patriot dream
> That sees, beyond the years,
> Thine alabaster cities gleam
> Undimmed by human tears!

Hardly a reality, you may say. Ah, but what a vision! Alabaster cities gleaming somewhere down the shining road of the future. Poverty and disease conquered. War abolished. People living joyous lives of work and play and service, no tears. If Frémont could dream his impossible dreams and have them realized 150 years later, who knows what may happen to our own dreams and images in another century or two?

But there are some pressing problems that we have to solve first. And one of these concerns the ancient and honorable estate known as matrimony. Let us devote this chapter to a discussion of marriage and where it stands today.

Everyone knows that the divorce rate in this country has risen to the point where, in some states at least, one out of every two marriages winds up as a failure. This is a deeply disturbing state of affairs, because marriage is the glue that holds the family together—and the family is the basic unit of society, indeed of civilization itself. Cicero said, "The empire is at the fireside."

What is the matter with modern marriage, anyway? I think the answer is that there is nothing wrong with marriage. What is wrong is the concept—that is to say, the image—of marriage that has prevailed in the last two or three decades, especially among our young people.

The other day, on a shuttle plane between Boston and New York, I found myself sitting beside an affable stranger. When I casually asked him what took him to New York, he said that he was going down to attend his daughter's wedding that afternoon.

"Well, congratulations," I said. "That's wonderful."

He gave a wry little laugh. "Yes, a bit monotonous, though. This is her third."

"Oh!" I said, not knowing what else to say.

"She's a bright girl," he told me. "She has a very good job. But here she is, at the age of twenty-four, trying matrimony for the third time. Two down, and one to go. I hope this time it works."

"I hope so, too," I said.

"But you know," he went on a bit grimly. "I don't know why it should. This fellow she is marrying seems nice enough.

But so did the other two young fellows whom she divorced. This one's been divorced himself, and he's only twenty-five. I don't know what is happening to the institution of marriage, really. Young people nowadays seem to regard it as a kind of game of musical chairs." He stared out the window at the carpet of clouds below us and shook his head slowly. "It is a funny feeling to be going to your daughter's third wedding and saying to yourself, 'Maybe it'll work and maybe it won't.'"

"Maybe," I said dryly, "that is where the trouble lies— in that word *maybe*."

And it does, you know. Let me explain.

Having been completely and happily married for a lot of years, I know I tend to look at marriage from a point of view that must seem pretty old-fashioned to some members of the younger generation. I believe in monogamy, fidelity, total commitment to a married partner. I believe in these things because the Word of God Himself tells us that that is the way human beings are supposed to live. And He certainly knows the score.

Ruth and I know from firsthand experience that the rewards of living that way are so great that any deviation seems just plain senseless. To us, marriage is a compact sealed with love that cannot be broken. It is a promise between two consenting adults to join their lives and stick together through thick and thin, good times and bad, until life comes to an end. No *maybe* about it for us. None whatsoever.

But in the last two or three decades that word has crept into the American concept of marriage until it is the word most often used.

The Fatal *Maybe* Attitude

"I'm getting married, and I hope it works, but maybe it won't. And if it doesn't, maybe I can just cancel out and look for another partner. Why not? That is what everybody's doing."

"I am married, but maybe I've made a mistake. Maybe

I've married a bit beneath me. Maybe I'm still growing and my partner has stopped growing. Maybe our sex life isn't what it ought to be. Maybe I'd be happier married to someone else. Maybe I'd be happier not married to anyone. . . ."

Maybe. Maybe. Maybe. Every single one of those *maybes* is a form of negative imaging. They represent images of marital failure. They leave an escape hatch always open. And the more they are thought about, or toyed with, or dwelled upon, the stronger is the possibility that the escape hatch will be used.

Two or three years ago, a young woman came to me saying that her husband was neglecting her. He was a brilliant young medical student, but she complained that he studied day and night. He never took her out to a play or a movie. He never took her dancing. They seldom went to a restaurant. They barely had enough money for necessities, and none for luxuries. He had his nose in a book all the time.

She went on whining like this for several minutes. Finally she said, "I don't know why I married Tom. There was another boy named Gerald who wanted to marry me, too. I turned him down for Tom, but I made a mistake. Maybe I should have married Gerald—"

"Stop," I said to her. "Stop right there. Your husband isn't neglecting you, young lady; you're neglecting him. He is working his heart out trying to prepare for a life of helping people. He needs all the support he can get from a loyal, loving wife, not sulks and tantrums from a spoiled little fluffy kitten. So my advice to you is this: Go back to your husband. Thank God every day of your life that you are fortunate enough to be married to a man like that. Put all these ridiculous *maybes* out of your mind. The one *maybe* you can use would be to say to yourself, 'Maybe I can think of a new way to be loving and supportive of Tom today.'"

Harsh words? Perhaps. But she needed to hear them. She went away looking very pensive, and evidently some of the words got through to her, because she is still married to Tom, not to Gerald or anyone else, and Tom is about ready to start a successful medical career. Parenthetically I suggested to Tom that he knock off once in a while and at least go to McDonald's for a Big Mac. He did, and they both had fun.

Young people are not the only ones who have a flawed concept of marriage these days. Ruth and I receive a great deal of mail from older people struggling with marital difficulties, and a remarkably high percentage deals with a phenomenon that we sometimes refer to as the Walkaway Husband Problem. In letter after letter, bewildered, unhappy, heartbroken women report that after fifteen, twenty, even thirty years of marriage their life partner has suddenly walked out on them. Sometimes another woman is involved; sometimes not. Sometimes the husbands give an explanation; sometimes they don't. The net result is the same: The husband, often the chief breadwinner, is suddenly no longer there, leaving a wife and often children to struggle as best they can to rebuild their lives, or even to survive.

Again it seems plain to me that behind this grim and increasingly frequent state of affairs lies a faulty image of marriage. To the walkaway husband, marriage has become the symbol of a relationship full of drudgery, monotony, and unrequited sacrifice. He sees himself as the plodding, patient, long-suffering bearer of endless financial burdens. *All these years*, he tells himself, *I've been pulling this load. Ninety-five percent of my earnings have gone to support this wife and these children. But what about me?*

What does he have to show for all this effort? A wife who's overweight physically and underweight mentally. Children who are leaving the nest, who have their own lives to lead. As time goes by, he and his wife have less and less in common, less and less to talk about. Here he is, at age fifty, or fifty-five. He probably has a couple of pretty good decades left. He thinks, *Why don't I get out from under these burdens and live a little? Maybe I'll meet some woman who is physically more attractive and mentally more stimulating.* Who knows, instead of being totally dependent on him, she might be a strong person who could help him to cope with problems—a partner instead of a drag! "Anyway," he says, "I've had it. I've done my duty. I've served my time. I'm getting out!"

And to the consternation of everyone—wife, children, friends, neighbors—out he goes.

The sad thing about these cases is that I'm sure they never happen overnight. Almost always the discontent of the husband (or of the wife if the situation is reversed) has been growing over a long period of time, and the discontented partner has been giving warning signals of all kinds. "For heaven's sake, Agnes, stop nagging me about going to church!" "Harold, why don't you talk to me anymore? All you do is come home and drink beer and stare at the television!"

The signals are clear enough. But they are ignored. Communication fades away. Neither partner is willing or able to look realistically at his or her own performance, or share the blame for the slow deterioration that is taking place. And so they pass the point of no return and slide faster and faster down the slope that ends in desertion or divorce.

Now, what is the remedy for all this? What can be done to prevent such dismal endings to once-bright hopes and dreams? What can people whose marriage is in trouble do about it?

I think the main thing they can do is try to revive and recapture the image of marriage as a triumphant, rewarding, lifelong partnership where the pluses outweigh the minuses by an overwhelming margin. I think they have to stop focusing on the worst aspects of their lives together and reach out for the best—expect it and hope for it and pray for it and work for it and image it until it once more becomes a reality.

I sometimes think it would help if ministers who marry starry-eyed young couples would urge them to project themselves into the future, see themselves raising a happy houseful of kids, visualize themselves working out problems together as a team in human service, supporting each other, loving each other, being faithful to each other. They should be encouraged to visualize their later years, with grandchildren coming along and a great and satisfying marriage parntership growing ever closer and more loving. They should be urged to paint this dream as vividly as possible, and they should be assured that the reality would follow the dream if they imaged it and worked for it and prayed for it hard enough.

Imaging? Of course. But it really does create a climate in which an ever-deepening relationship can grow and flourish.

Experiment Saved a Marriage

Imaging can also be a healing influence in marriages where cracks have appeared. Some years ago a couple I had married wrote to me saying that things were going badly and that they were on the verge of divorce. They thought that since I had married them, they should let me know.

In my reply I urged them to carry out a week-long experiment that I said might save their tottering marriage. I told them to find an alarm clock, one with a loud tick, then each morning go into a room with two chairs and spend twenty minutes in uninterrupted silence.

In the first ten minutes, I wanted each of them to visualize in vivid detail (it was imaging, but I didn't call it that) what their lives would be like after the divorce. The effect on the children. The loneliness. The guilt. The sense of loss and broken dreams. The financial strains and dislocations. The side taking among former friends. The whole dreary aftermath.

Then in the second ten minutes, I urged them to recall as vividly as possible some of the happiest, most loving times they had known together. Imaging again: the memory of past happiness can point the compass of the unconscious mind toward the goal of similar happiness in the future.

I told them, finally, that if they would listen carefully to the loud, rhythmic tick of the clock, they would find it repeating the word that was at the bottom of all their troubles: *self, self, self, self!* I urged them both to ask the Lord to come into their hearts and remove that most universal of all sins: selfishness. If they would do that, I told them, they would be praying together. And I added that never in all my experience had I known any couple to get a divorce who had prayed together.

Well, you know, it worked. And imaging had a lot to do with it.

I remember other cases, too, where imaging saved a shaky marriage. In World War II, many marriages underwent severe strains when there were long separations, wives alone at home, soldier-husbands far away overseas. In one fairly typical case, a young husband stationed in England fell in love with an American Red Cross girl who was also stationed there. When the war ended, the soldier came back to his wife and told her that he was sorry, but he had met another girl, they had fallen in love, they were sure they were made for each other. He said he felt very badly about the way things had worked out, especially since he and his wife had two small children born before the war, but he wanted his wife to give him a divorce. He was sure that, under the circumstances, she would.

But the wife had had a Quaker upbringing, which meant that she had a quiet inner strength. She did not panic. She did not fly into a jealous rage. She told her husband that she knew him better than he knew himself. He was, she said, basically a good father and a good husband. That side of him would reassert itself someday. Until that day, she would simply wait. She would not give him a divorce.

The husband argued, he pleaded, he told the wife that he no longer loved her, that he loved the Red Cross girl. He said that by refusing to let him go, she was making them all miserable. He added that, being young and attractive, his wife would undoubtedly marry again. She replied that she already had a marriage. It was going through a difficult period, she admitted, but sooner or later it would come out the other side, stronger than before. She could see that day clearly in her mind. She visualized the two of them going on with their lives, raising their children, and perhaps having more. She imaged them in love again, this whole dark interlude forgotten. She said serenely that she believed this was God's plan for them. Therefore, she could not give him a divorce.

The husband departed, angry and frustrated. He went back to the Red Cross girl, who was waiting for him in her hometown. He told her that his wife would eventually stop being so stubborn. It was just a matter of time. He was in a difficult and humiliating position. All they had to do was wait.

So they waited. And waited. And waited. And gradually it became apparent to the Red Cross girl that *she* was the one who was in the humiliating position. Finally she told her lover that she was tired of waiting for the stubborn wife to step aside. The glamour was gone from their situation. She wanted a husband of her own, not a man anchored to another woman. She told him to get lost.

By this time the husband was beginning to have second thoughts himself. As his wife had said, there was a part of him that recognized his obligations to her and the children. And he also became increasingly conscious of deep emotional ties that he knew existed. He was impressed that his wife was really a great woman. Finally, sheepishly and contritely, he came back home. His wife welcomed him quietly. She was not surprised. It was all working out just the way she had imaged it. There were no recriminations. She took him back. And that marriage went forward successfully, saved by the emotional balance and good sense of a real woman who imaged her way through an ugly situation and came out triumphantly on the other side.

I remember another case in a small town where a woman was married to a man who was a notorious philanderer. He was very attractive to women, and whenever temptation crossed his path he followed Oscar Wilde's advice to get rid of the temptation by giving in to it. Small towns being what they are, his affairs and escapades were common knowledge, and from time to time certain ladies of the community, pillars of society themselves, of course, would decide that it was their duty to tell the wife about the misdeeds of her husband.

She Imaged Her Marriage to Success

But they never got much satisfaction when they did. The wife would smile and shake her head and say that she knew they meant well, but they were mistaken. She knew her husband. She trusted him. She knew he loved her. It was impossible for her to conceive of any such disloyalty on his part. Her informants were simply misinformed. The informants would go away baffled and frustrated, because they knew very well that they were right.

Now, was this wife actually imaging a husband who was a model of marital fidelity, or was she just being remarkably patient and wise? Being a mere man, I can't answer that question. All I know is that gradually the amorous adventures of the husband began to be less frequent. Finally they ceased altogether. And when a close friend asked him, in considerable amazement, what had happened, the husband said, "Well, you know, when my wife trusted me and refused to believe what people told her, even when it was true, I began to feel more and more like a low-down, no-good skunk. If she loved me that much, then the least I could do was to try to live up to her concept of me. And that's what I'm going to do from now on."

In other words, the man responded to the image of himself that he saw reflected in his wife's eyes—and began behaving like a man-sized husband instead of a heel.

Even when a clear, steady image of successful marriage is kept in mind, it is a relationship that must be constantly monitored, adjusted, and nourished. Here are seven suggestions that Ruth and I recommend to marriage partners who want to keep the flame alive.

1. *Try to have a mature concept of what love really is.* For too many Americans, love is a breathless romantic glow in which they expect to have their own emotional needs gratified. Some people, especially young people, are really little more than receiving stations for this kind of supportive attention from a member of the opposite sex. They are addicted to it. They have to have it, and they sulk if they don't get it.

But this is dependency, not love. It is shallow, not deep. It is a feeling, not a commitment, a feeling that can change as moods or circumstances change—and if the feeling vanishes, even temporarily, then it is easy to decide that love has ended.

Romantic love doesn't really change anyone. Mature love

has a spiritual dimension that alters a person profoundly, and changes him or her from a self-oriented person to an others-oriented person. In mature love, the beloved's welfare and happiness becomes more important than your own; as someone said, real love is the accurate estimate and supply of another's needs. Another definition: Love is what comes from living through difficulties together. These concepts are a long way from the romantic, sex-saturated depiction of love that is so prevalent and so popular in our American culture. But they are far closer to the truth.

Some people never learn that love is not just a pleasant feeling; it is a way of regarding another person and treating that person. A young woman sitting stony-faced in my office not long ago said to me, "I don't love my husband anymore."

I said, "How do you know that?"

She said, "I don't feel loving toward him, that's why. I don't feel anything."

I said, "Love is more than a feeling. If for one month you will simply do the loving thing where your husband is concerned, do it regardless of how you feel or don't feel, perhaps the affection you once had for him will come back. Act as though you love him, whether you think you do or not. The important thing right now is how you act, not how you feel. If you will make yourself do the loving thing, if you will simply treat your husband with kindness and consideration, you may be able to salvage your marriage."

To act in this way is not deception. It is the dramatization, really, of a hoped-for image of things to come. In this case, that woman is still trying, and successfully, too, for the marriage is still alive.

2. *Work on communications constantly.* No matter how long you have been married, you can never take your lines of communication for granted. They need to be constantly used, tested, and if necessary repaired.

If a husband and wife are separated during most of the day, as many couples are, it is wise to set aside a specific time, perhaps early in the morning, perhaps before going to bed, to talk about plans and problems, grievances or misunderstandings, all or any aspect of living together. That way, difficulties can be dealt with while they are still molehills, not mountains. Once the habit of sharing things verbally is established, the marriage becomes much more resistant to the stress and strains that surround it.

The truth is, marriage is a contract that needs to be renegotiated constantly, with compromises and concessions and common sense. You have to watch for areas where you are *not* communicating (for example, can each partner discuss in-laws frankly and openly?) and try to get a dialogue going.

There are many forms of communication in marriage. Sometimes sympathetic listening is the best form; sometimes just knowing when to be silent. Sometimes it is working together; sometimes it is shared play. Sometimes it is a casual, affectionate touch; sometimes just a glance. Sometimes shared laughter. Sometimes the joy of sexual reunion. Whatever form it takes, it is the heartbeat of marriage. When it ceases, the marriage dies.

3. *Learn how to defer gratification*. This is a combination of self-control and patience. Both marriage partners have to be willing at times to put off or forgo immediate pleasures or satisfaction in order to obtain greater benefits in the future. This may sound obvious, but I have seen the failure to do this wreck many marriages. Some people cannot bring themselves to save money, or put it to work for them in long-range plans or investments. Others refuse to work overtime, even when overtime work will ultimately bring them significant rewards. They're too interested in having their pleasure or their recreation right now.

Imaging helps here, too, because if you image a desired goal vividly enough, if you visualize the rewards of patience and self-discipline clearly enough, you can often supply the motivation that otherwise might be missing.

I often think that if quarreling couples on the brink of divorce would just defer *that* gratification for a few weeks or months, they might wind up with a stronger marriage than before. They might learn that difficulties or even pain can be a trigger to growth. They might even realize, upon reflection, that escaping out the back door of marriage is not likely to change the basic problems they are facing;

those problems will probably go right along with them into the next relationship that they try to establish.

4. *Take responsibility.* Accept the truth that marriage is going to be what you and one other person make it, no better and no worse. Face up to the fact that in any disagreement or controversy you are not going to change your partner very much, if at all. The only person you can really change is yourself. But when you do change yourself, by accepting blame occasionally, by apologizing sometimes, by compromising now and then, the whole human equation changes and things often work out the way you want after all.

A man said to me not long ago, "I prayed about my wife's drinking problem."

"Has she stopped drinking?" I asked.

"No," he said, "but I've stopped nagging her. I've stopped thinking about leaving her. I think I've found the strength to go on living with her and loving her no matter what. I believe I have found the patience to lead her to the help she needs. And someday I think she will change."

I think so, too. As some wise person said, "Prayer doesn't necessarily change things for you, but it changes you for things."

5. *Learn to compromise.* Compromise doesn't mean giving in. It just means that you recognize that there are two (or more) sides to every question. Sometimes it helps to trade a bit, in a good-humored way. If the husband will go to church on Sunday instead of playing golf, the wife will stop smoking. If he will stop leaving the ice trays unfilled, she will stop squeezing the toothpaste tube in the middle. That sort of thing.

When Ruth and I first bought a place in the country over thirty years ago, she loved the house but I was bothered by the fact that across the road was a huge barn that cut off a part of our view. Ruth kept telling me how picturesque it was, but still it bothered me. It bothered me, in fact, for the next twenty-one years. Then another house became available one-half mile away where there was nothing to obstruct the view. By now Ruth was devoted to the house we had, but she knew how I felt about that barn. She felt that she had had her "druthers" for twenty-one years; now it was time for me to have mine. And so, gracefully, she agreed to move. Compromise—lubricating oil in the machinery of marriage! Footnote: She now loves the house we moved to.

6. *Practice the art of appreciation.* Everybody cherishes a word of praise. Some psychologists believe that the desire for approval is one of the strongest human traits, maybe even *the* strongest. So why not master the art of the casual compliment, the little unforeseen gesture that says, "I think you're wonderful just the way you are"? An unexpected bouquet of flowers. A love note in a pocket or under a pillow.

It was Arnold Bennett, I believe, who remarked (in his bachelor days) that it seemed to him that marriage nearly always resulted in the death of politeness between man and wife. But that doesn't have to be the case. Try complimenting your wife or your husband just once a day. The resulting rush of affection will surprise you. If they don't die of astonishment first!

7. *Strive always to increase the spiritual dimension of your life together.* Marriage is a difficult and demanding relationship; people in it need all the help they can get. A simple and extremely practical rule is to keep Christ in the center of your life, and decisions will be sounder, joys will be greater, troubles will be more bearable, burdens will seem lighter. One businessman said a surprising and unexpected thing to me: "When I'm away from home, I call my wife long-distance every night. And when I do, I try to visualize God as a third person listening in, sharing our problems, understanding our needs, watching over both of us. It is a kind of prayer, I guess. Anyway, we both get a lot of good out of it."

Of course they do. And so do married couples who pray together, go to church together, read the Bible together, believe together. There is a Bible passage that sums it up: "Except the Lord build the house, they labour in vain that build it" (Psalms 127:1).

I once heard a wise marriage counselor compare marriage to the base camp that mountain climbers establish when they plan the conquest of some mighty peak like the Matterhorn or Mount Everest. The mountain represents life itself. The base camp of marriage is the place where the climbers—the marriage partners—keep the supplies and equipment that are essential to their assault on the mountain.

The base camp really represents survival; if at a temporary camp at higher elevations something goes wrong, the climbers can always retreat to the base camp to find food and warmth and shelter, to renew their strength for another attempt. There is liberty for each of the climbers to go forth and try different routes to the summit. But the base camp is where communication takes place, where plans and decisions are made. Unless the base camp functions as it is intended to function, the expedition will fail.

So if you are married, or if you ever intend to be married, hold in your mind the image of a base camp well and truly chosen, equipped with love and companionship, warmed by loyalty and faith and trust. And never forget to ask God's blessings on all comings and goings. Then venture with confidence to climb the highest peaks that life can offer.

11
The Healing Power of Forgiveness

Usually, when it comes time on Sunday morning for me to speak, I have gone over the material so often and so carefully that it is pretty well fixed in my mind. By the time church begins at 11:15 A.M., this process of preparation is supposed to be over. But one Sunday morning recently I was having trouble with a talk as late as 10:45 A.M. I needed an illustration for a certain point, and I didn't have one, and I couldn't think of one, and the clock was ticking, and I was getting more and more uneasy.

Sitting at the desk in my study, I happened to look up at the top of the bookcase, and there was a little toy coal scuttle filled with miniature lumps of toy coal. That coal scuttle, complete with toy shovel, had been sitting there for at least thirty years, and I had ceased to be aware of it. But there was the illustration I needed!

Thirty years ago I was called to see a patient in a hospital. This woman had had a lot of misfortune in her life. Some people had treated her very badly. They had cheated her and lied to her and almost ruined her, and she hated them. This hatred darkened all her thoughts and colored them a deep, funereal black. And this in turn had begun to affect her health. She told me that she was in and out of hospitals all the time which, under the circumstances, was not surprising. She wanted me to help her.

Well, I tried, but didn't have much success. I told her that she would have to forgive the people she believed had wronged her, but she said she couldn't do this. Her feelings of anger and resentment had gained such a grip on her mind that it was impossible to displace them. Even when I told her that these thoughts were probably the cause of all her health problems, she seemed unable to relinquish them. She just went on seething with anger. She said it was justifiable anger, and maybe it was, but it was destroying her nevertheless.

One day, looking for Christmas presents for my own children, I happened to see the little toy coal scuttle, and at once this woman and her problems came to mind. So I bought the coal scuttle and took it around to her at the hospital. "Here is a present for you," I told her. "But it is more than a present, it is a prescription that may help you overcome all these health problems. I know you hate the people who wronged you, but hate is a boomerang and some of it is circling back and hurting you."

I took the toy shovel and scooped out some of the toy coal. "Those hate thoughts are as hard and black as these little lumps of toy coal," I said. "So, whenever one of these ugly thoughts comes into your mind, take this little shovel and lift out a little black lump of coal and throw it under the bed, out of sight. As you do this, visualize the dark thought being cast out of your consciousness. The more black thoughts you throw out of your mind, the sooner your mind will return to its original coloration, which is not black, but clean and white. And once your mind is normal and healthy, your body will become normal and healthy, too."

I remember she looked at the little toy coal scuttle and laughed. "You must be joking," she said. Then she added slowly, "But the way I've been feeling is no joke, is it? All right. I'll try it."

"Fine," I said. "And when the lumps of coal are all gone, have your nurse sweep them up, and start all over again."

She did, and apparently was able to make the transference between this simple symbolic act and the deeper healing process that she needed so badly, because gradually she began to get better. She no longer spent time in hospital beds. She became a well woman, a strong, practicing Christian who lived without the poison of hate in her mind or heart. Finally, she gave me back the little coal scuttle, saying that it had done its job. I put it up on the bookcase, and there it stayed until I needed it for my sermon that morning, which was on the healing power of forgiveness.

One of the most important lessons that people can learn as they move through life is how to forgive. Our Lord told us to forgive our enemies, not once, not seven times, but seventy times seven. Maybe He smiled as He said it, but the fact that He talked about forgiveness in such terms shows that He recognized how hard forgiving someone who has wronged you can be. It is difficult, hideously difficult, yet over and over again Jesus stressed how important it is. He even said that if you have a quarrel with someone, it is useless to bring a gift to God's altar and ask for blessings until you first go and seek reconciliation with that person. Anger, resentment, and hatred set up barriers that deprive a person of spiritual power. Chronic malevolence, smoldering anger, or some terrible and long-lasting grudge are not unlike cancerous growths.

So forgiveness is not just a nice praiseworthy virtue that one ought to display because it is the Christian thing to do. Forgiveness is a needed protection for yourself. It is an antidote for poisons that can corrupt the body and damage the soul.

Compassionate Judgment

How do you set about becoming a forgiving individual? First you decide by an act of will that you are not going to be a judgmental person. The Bible says quite clearly, "Judge not . . ." (Matthew 7:1), and the reason behind this prohibition is plain: We never have all the information that would enable us to make an absolutely just judgment. There are always some things that are hidden from us, things known only to God. So it is better to leave the judging to Him. If punishment is necessary, let Him take care of it. "Vengeance is mine; I will repay, saith the Lord." In any case, none of us is so perfect that we can afford to be harsh and totally unforgiving of people whose actions hurt or displease us.

I will admit that it takes a good many years of living before you begin to see this clearly. People sometimes ask Ruth and me if our approach to helping people with their problems has changed much over the years. Well, not a great deal, but I do think we are a little more tolerant, a little more compassionate than when we started out. We know that human beings are going to make mistakes, because they are just that—human beings. And besides, we make a few mistakes ourselves. We have also learned that each of us is a tremendously delicate and complicated piece of machinery, subject to all sorts of hidden strains and stresses, and when you look at all the factors in a given case you can't help wondering how, by and large, people do as well as they do.

Some months ago, for example, I found myself talking with a woman who had consulted me because she was in deep trouble. She worked for an insurance company, and she had been stealing money from the company by falsifying insurance claims. By forging the names of doctors and inventing medical events that never happened, she had swindled the company out of almost fifty thousand dollars. She was terrified that company officials would become suspicious and start an investigation. Remorseful and frightened, she turned to me for help.

Now the woman was a thief, no doubt about that. Confession was inevitable. Restitution had to be made. And yet I think my own reaction was a bit different from what it might have been thirty years ago. Then I might have reacted mainly with righteous indignation. "You've stolen money," I might have said. "We had better go to the authorities right now. Right is right and wrong is wrong. You have stepped over the line and now you must bear the consequences."

But through the years I have learned to listen more and judge less. This distracted woman, I learned, had had a hysterectomy at twenty-six, an early age, thereby losing her capacity ever to become a mother. I began to see that her compulsive desire to acquire material things—which in turn had led her to defraud her own company—was a pathetic attempt to compensate for the children she could never have. I didn't excuse what she had done. But I did feel sorry for her.

So, after talking it over with Ruth, I called up a good friend of mine in the insurance business, described the case to him, and asked him what he thought we should do. He said that in his opinion the woman should go to the president of her company, or the highest official she could reach, confess what she had done, and ask for forgiveness and the chance to repay the money bit by bit. "I think they may be fairly lenient with her," my friend said. "The sum that seems so large to her is not that large to them. From what you say, this woman is truly sorry and wants to make amends. It may be that civil authority will not have to be brought into it."

So that was the course we followed, and in the end it did work out the way my friend predicted. The point is, a young woman who made a bad mistake was spared a criminal record because Ruth and I had learned to be more tolerant and—I hope—more understanding over the years.

A sense of compassion, then, and a conscious refusal to be a judgmental person are the first steps toward acquiring a capacity for forgiveness. Even so, it remains a difficult attitude to achieve when you think you are wronged. The instinctive, animalistic reaction is to fight back, to inflict hurt because you have been hurt. But this is precisely the response that Jesus was trying to eliminate from our hearts when He told us to love our enemies and "do good to those who despitefully use you" (*see* Matthew 5:44).

He told us that because He knew that forgiveness liberates enormous healing powers in both the forgiver and the forgiven. Recently I heard of a doctor in New York, a cancer specialist, who is very highly regarded in his field. When a new patient comes to him, before he starts any kind of treatment this doctor tries to find out all he can about the patient's background, especially relationships with parents, brothers and sisters, and any close relative or very close friend. He believes that emotional factors play a large part in a person's susceptibility to cancer, and makes a point of trying to understand the emotional climate in which the disease began.

One of the things this physician does is summon all members of the family to a session which he calls the Hour of Forgiveness. In this rather extraordinary meeting, each person is asked to express openly any grievance or resentment that he or she may have been carrying toward the patient, or even toward one another. Then, when these hidden animosities are brought out, the owner of them is asked quite simply to forgive the offender, or the fancied offender. In these sessions, amazing things come to light and often are resolved then and there.

Once these hidden grievances are neutralized by the power of forgiveness, the doctor calls for one more session called the Hour of Love, in which everyone involved expresses affection and concern for everyone else. First forgiveness. Then love. The result, this remarkable doctor feels, is an atmosphere in which the healing forces he intends to apply will work most effectively. And I think this must often be the case.

How does imaging come into all this? In a variety of ways. If you are at odds with a friend, it certainly helps to visualize that quarrel ended, the old relationship restored, the sense of pain and alienation eliminated. If you can fix that image in your mind, you have taken a tremendous first step.

If the feelings of anger and resentment go very deep, sometimes it may help to image clearly and vividly the face of the person who has wronged you, then picture the face of Jesus as you imagine it looks, then superimpose that image of Christ on top of the other image and say out loud, "I forgive you in the Name of Jesus. Amen." This is a healing prayer and a powerful one. The *Amen* at the end means "so be it," and it is really a command to your own subconscious to let go of the negative, punitive thoughts that have sunk their roots so deep into your mind. Pull them out, throw them away for good.

Prayer is necessary because sometimes forgiveness is so difficult that we simply cannot do it alone. It assuredly requires the grace of God to come into our mind and change it before we can even begin to change ourselves. But when God's power and love are allowed to act as a solvent, even the deepest bitterness can be washed away. And this is a fact, believe me.

Inspiring Story of Two Families

A few years ago in Pennsylvania, there was a sturdy farming family consisting of Jay, his wife, Ruth, and three fine sons, the youngest a cheerful, freckle-faced schoolboy named Nelson. His teachers called him "Sunshine" because he had such a lovable disposition and such a sunny smile. One day when Jay and Ruth were waiting for Nelson to come home from school, the school-bus driver came running, frantic and white-faced, up the lane. Nelson had been hit by a car as he was getting off the school bus. An ambulance was summoned, but it was too late. Nelson was dead.

The driver of the car was an off-duty policeman from New York City. With his wife he had been driving through the tranquil Pennsylvania countryside. The school bus had stopped; its warning lights and stop sign were functioning. But somehow this driver ignored them. He tried to pass the bus. And little Nelson was killed.

Jay and Ruth were devastated. So were their other sons. Their neighbors were enraged; they wanted the harshest penalties invoked. School authorities wanted to make an example of the guilty driver, an outsider, a big-city stranger.

The days went by in a blur of grief and anguish. An insurance adjuster came to discuss settlements. He had also been in touch with the policeman and his wife, and something prompted Jay to ask how they were.

"They seem broken up," the insurance man told him.

Broken up. Ruth and Jay knew what those words meant; they meant the other couple was miserable, too. They thought about it, talked about it, prayed about it. Finally they decided to ask the New York couple, whose names were Frank and Rose Ann, to come to their house for dinner. And they came.

It was awkward, of course. But the four grieving people sat down and broke bread together. Ruth and Jay learned that Frank had been a policeman for eight years and had a spotless record. The accident, he said, might cost him his job. He and Rose Ann, like Ruth and Jay, had three children. They had sent them to Rose Ann's parents because they were fearful of facing their neighbors. Both Frank and Rose Ann looked terrible. There were dark circles under their eyes. They had lost a great deal of weight.

After they left, Ruth and Jay sat down at the kitchen table and faced each other. They faced something else, too: the fact that Frank and Rose Ann were suffering almost as much as they were. The truth became plain that only through compassion, only through applying the kind of love that their religion stood for, only through forgiveness offered and accepted, could all of them find peace. And so when the trial was held, Jay decided not to press charges. Except for a traffic fine, Frank was free.

Forgiveness. What is it, really? Perhaps it is no more than the opportunity to try again, to do better, to be freed from the penalties and shackles of past mistakes. Whatever it is, it's something we all need and long for. That is why our hearts are touched and our eyes grow misty when we encounter truly great examples of it.

I remember a remarkable story of forgiveness told more than twenty years ago by Bob Considine, the famous Hearst newspaper reporter. It concerned a government warehouse worker named Karl Taylor and his wife, Edith. The Taylors had been married for twenty-three years, and they seemed a devoted couple. Whenever Karl's job took him out of town, he would write Edith a long letter every night and send small gifts from every place he visited.

In 1949 the government sent Karl to Okinawa for a few months to work on a warehouse there. Left alone in the little Massachusetts town of Waltham, Edith made the best of it as the slow months went by. She kept herself busy buying a little unfinished cottage and trying to get it completed as a surprise for Karl when he came home.

But Karl kept delaying, and letters became fewer. Finally, after weeks of silence, a note came from Karl: "Dear Edith, I wish I knew of a kinder way to tell you that we are no longer married. . . ." Karl had written to Mexico for a divorce. He had obtained one by mail. He told Edith he was going to marry a young Japanese girl named Aiko, a maid who had been assigned to his quarters. She was nineteen. Edith was forty-eight.

Edith had every reason to be embittered and crushed. By all the laws of human nature, she should have hated the Japanese woman and despised Karl. But somehow this didn't happen. Perhaps Edith was so full of love for Karl that she simply could not hate him. In any case, she was able to understand what had happened. A lonely man, far from home, who sometimes drank too much. A penniless, vulnerable girl.

Even in her grief, Edith tried to find something good in Karl's behavior. At least he had the honesty to get a divorce and marry the girl. He hadn't abandoned Aiko. Edith didn't really think the marriage would work out. There was too much dissimilarity in age and background. Someday Aiko and Karl would discover this. Then perhaps Karl would come home. She sold the little cottage she had worked on so long and so hard. She never told Karl about it. She kept on working at her factory job. And she waited.

But Karl never came home. He wrote to Edith saying that he and Aiko were expecting a baby. Marie was born in 1951, then another girl, Helen, in 1953. Edith sent the children little presents. She went on with her factory job in Waltham, but the real focus of her life was on Okinawa.

Then one day a terrible letter came: Karl was dying of lung cancer. The letter was full of fear, not so much for himself as for Aiko and the two children. His medical expenses were draining away his savings. What would become of them?

Edith knew, then, what she wanted to do. Her last gift to Karl could be a measure of peace of mind. She wrote and told him that she would take the two children to live with her in Massachusetts.

Aiko was their mother, and she didn't want to let them go. But what could she offer them, except poverty and hopelessness? In 1956 she finally agreed. The children were sent to Edith. They adjusted quickly to American ways, and Edith was happier than she had been for many years.

But Aiko, alone on Okinawa, was miserable. She wrote pathetic notes to Edith: "Aunt. Tell me what they do. If Marie or Helen cry or not." Finally Edith knew that there was one more thing her love for Karl would require. She would bring the children's mother to her home, too.

It was not easy. Aiko was still a Japanese citizen and the immigration quota was full, with many waiting. But Edith Taylor wrote to Bob Considine, asking his aid. He told the story in his newspaper column. Others helped. Finally, in 1957, Aiko was permitted to enter the United States.

Here is how Bob Considine described the meeting that took place:

As the plane came in at New York's International Airport, Edith had a moment of fear. What if she should hate this woman who had taken Karl away from her?

The last person off the plane was a girl so thin and small Edith thought at first it was a child. She did not come down the stairs, she only stood there, clutching the railing, and Edith knew that if she had been afraid, Aiko was near panic.

She called Aiko's name and the girl rushed down the steps and into Edith's arms. In that brief moment, as they held each other, Edith had an extraordinary thought. "Help me," she said, her eyes shut tight. "Help me to love this girl, as if she were part of Karl, come home. I prayed for him to come back. Now he has—in his two little daughters and in this gentle girl that he loved. Help me, God, to know that."

I'm told Edith and Aiko Taylor still live together today, having raised Karl's two children, who are now fine young women. Why does this story of selflessness and forgiveness touch us so? Because there is a kind of divinity in it. "Father, forgive them . . . ," said Jesus on the cross (Luke 23:34).

That is the model, the perfect example that is always before us. But only a very few, like Edith Taylor, come close to living up to it.

If, then, you want to experience the happiness, relief, and well-being that come from the practice of forgiveness, remember these five steps:

1. *Resist the temptation to be judgmental.* Remember, only God knows all the circumstances. Leave the judging to Him.

2. *Learn to be compassionate.* The best method is to use your imagination, put yourself in the other person's shoes, ask yourself whether the fault is entirely the other person's or whether there is some blame on your own part that needs to be honestly faced.

3. *Image the whole problem in terms of reconciliation.* Visualize the broken relationship healed. See yourself freed of the poisons of resentment and anger. Let your imagination suggest hopeful things you will accomplish with the increased energy that will come to you.

4. *Pray for the person who has offended you.* If this is difficult (and it will be), pray for God's grace to come into your heart to give you the strength to do it. Remind yourself that the act of forgiveness will benefit you more than the other person.

5. *End your prayer with the Lord's prayer.* Give special thought and emphasis to the part that asks God to forgive us our debts as we forgive our debtors.

Do these five things and you will be amazed at the healing power of forgiveness. If you let it, it can change your life.

12
Imaging the Tenseness out of Tension

What is this thing called tension, this painful feeling called tension? It is not easy to define. Fear can cause it, but it's not exactly fear. Worry can cause it; so can guilt, hate, or frustration. One thing is sure: We all know the dismal feeling that comes when tension digs its claws into us. The sense of strain. The feelings of inadequacy. The pessimism. The low boiling point. "My nerves are shot," we say. "I'm uptight. I'm ready to climb the walls."

Certainly there is too much tension, too much uptightness in our lives; the prevalence of high blood pressure and the astronomical sales of tranquilizers attest to that. But a little of it can be a stimulus, even a good thing. Dr. Hans Selye, the famous Canadian authority on this problem, has proved beyond doubt that prolonged stress can cause all sorts of illness in rats—and in people. Yet even Dr. Selye admits that some stress is inevitable and even desirable if an organism is to meet the challenges of its environment successfully.

I know this from my own experience. Every time I deliver a sermon or make a speech, I feel some tension. Maybe it is a throwback to my old inferiority-complex days; maybe

127

it is some dim recollection of that small boy being dragged into the parlor to reluctantly recite poetry to visiting relatives. Whatever the cause, it's painful and I don't like it. And yet I know it is a kind of spur, goading me to give my best effort. Without tension, most of us would never rise to the potential that the good Lord put into us.

In this chapter I am not going to talk about this normal and desirable level of stress or tension. I'm going to talk about the kind of tension that hurts and cripples and limits people—and what can be done about it.

Years ago, I ran across a remedy for acute tension that I have been using and recommending ever since. It is a three-part remedy, and one of those parts involves imaging, although that word was not in use at the time.

Coming home one evening, tired and tense and uptight, I fell into my favorite chair and glanced at the table alongside the chair where my loving wife has a habit of leaving books or magazines or pamphlets that she thinks might interest me. This time she had left, among other things, an insurance brochure. I remember it had the word *you* on the cover in big red letters, and a picture of a hand with an accusatory finger pointing right at the reader. "You," it said, "are full of tension! You are uptight! You are just about ready to explode!" *Well*, I thought, *that is a pretty good description of the way I'm feeling, all right. Maybe I'd better see what else they have to say about uptightness.*

The pamphlet went on to say that to get rid of excess tension, you had to do three things. The first was to practice relaxation of the physical body. "Sag back in your chair," it said. "Start relaxing every muscle, beginning with your toes. Stretch out your legs, flex your ankles, try to push your toes right off your feet, then let everything go limp. Let your head fall back. Roll it around so that your neck muscles are loosened up. Let each hand fall on your knee and rest there as limp as a wet leaf on a log. Open your eyes wide, then pretend invisible weights are attached to your eyelids, slowly pulling them shut. Imagine a soft, gentle hand lightly touching your face, smoothing the tension lines away. Picture the tension draining out of your body, leaving it calm and peaceful and relaxed." This is what Smiley Blanton called relaxing muscle tensions.

"Now you are ready for the second stage, which is the relaxation of the mind. This requires an effort of concentrated imagination. See yourself alone in the north woods of upstate New York on a perfect summer's day. You are sitting with your back against a tree; you can feel the rough bark through your shirt. All around you is a forest of fir, spruce, and hemlock. The air is scented with balsam. You can hear a gentle wind sighing in the treetops. In the far distance, blue hills are outlined against a tranquil sky. That sky is mirrored in a gleaming lake whose unruffled surface is broken only by the occasional leap of a fish. The ripples spread outward and are gone. The warm sun falls on your face like a benediction. Somewhere a bird calls and another answers. In the silence that follows, the healing beauty of God's creation surrounds you. Your uptightness fades away, smaller, smaller, until it is completely gone. Tension is no more. You are at peace...."

The pamphlet called that kind of mind relaxing an exercise in concentrated imagination. And so it was. But it was also a good example of imaging.

The third part of the remedy involved a deliberate attempt to refresh the soul by recalling and meditating upon great passages and great promises from the Scriptures. I have often found that one of the best antidotes for uptightness is simply to recite aloud the Twenty-third Psalm. "Yea, though I walk through the valley of the shadow of death, I will fear no evil: for thou art with me; thy rod and thy staff they comfort me" (verse 4). They do indeed!

The more you read your Bible, the more you memorize parts of it, the more you let these fragments of ancient wisdom sink down into the depths of your being, the less vulnerable you will be to the fears and uncertainties and perplexities that are the causes of tension.

There are so many of these mighty spirit lifters! "Let not your heart be troubled: ye believe in God, believe also in me. In my Father's house are many mansions..." (John 14:1, 2). "Peace I leave with you, my peace I give unto you..." (verse 27). "Thou wilt keep him in perfect peace, whose mind is stayed on thee" (Isaiah 26:3). "Fear thou not; for I am with thee: be not dismayed . . ." (Isaiah 41:10).

The three-pronged message of that insurance brochure was plain: Somehow, no matter how much stress or tension surrounds you, you have to try to maintain an inner equanimity, an imperturbability that cannot be shaken by external circumstances, no matter how trying or painful they may be.

The poet Edwin Markham once wrote, "At the heart of the cyclone tearing the sky is a place of central calm." We don't have cyclones (the modern word is tornado) up in Pawling, New York, where Ruth and I have our old farmhouse. But we do have line storms, fierce tempests that sweep up the coast in late August or September and come raging over Quaker Hill where our house stands, howling like ten thousand furies.

Storm on Our Farm

I remember one such night when Ruth and I were sitting by the fire in our quiet family room. Outside a line storm was raging. The wind would seize the house and shake it the way a terrier shakes a rat. Everything would creak and groan. Then there would be a lull in which we could hear the old Seth Thomas clock on the mantel ticking away the seconds.

Finally the wind became so furious that I was afraid some of our big maples would blow down. Taking a flashlight, I staggered out into the gale. Pointing the beam of the flashlight upward, I could see the great branches writhing and twisting and flailing about. It was terrifying; I wondered if the roof might blow off the house. I fought my way back inside and said to Ruth: "This is a killer storm. I know we're going to lose some trees. If the wind gets any worse, this whole place could blow down!"

Ruth said nothing for a few seconds. Then she said calmly, "Listen to the clock."

So I did listen to the clock. *Ticktock*, it went. *Ticktock*. Unhurried. Unconcerned. *This old house has been here for 150 years*, it seemed to be saying. *It has weathered storms like this in the past, and it will weather others in the future.*

What are you so upset about? Everything's okay. Ticktock. Okay. Ticktock. Okay. Ticktock . . .

It is a little strange to think you can be handed peace of mind by a clock, but that is what happened to me that night.

Years ago, when stress or tension began to build up in me, sometimes I would take the family and escape to Atlantic City for a day or two. It was a restful place then, with nothing very strenuous to do. People would walk on the boardwalk or on the beach. If it was wintertime, solicitous hotel attendants would wrap you up in a blanket and put you in a steamer chair facing the ocean so that all you could see was the majestic surge of breakers rolling in and all you could hear was the sound of the surf and the sea gulls crying as they wheeled on white wings over the restless water.

I remember thinking on one occasion, *Why do I have to come back here to find this kind of tranquility? Why can't I take it away with me in my mind and summon it up whenever I need it—a week from now, or a month, or six months, or a year.* And I would try to do just that when the pressures of New York became unbearable. Imaging, that's what it was. The kind of imaging that enables you to reach out and touch tranquility in the midst of stress.

I wonder sometimes just when all this sense of strain and hurry, all this uptightness, took over the nation. I don't remember it as a boy growing up in the Midwest. People had problems, of course, but nervous tension was seldom one of them. There was something soothing about the tempo of life, the horse-drawn wagons and the early automobiles, the placid shops and the quiet restaurants (no fast-food places, no drive-ins), the little country churches with the corn ("corn knee-high by the Fourth of July") reaching almost to the front door and then stretching away like an emerald ocean to the horizon, the clouds like fat, white sheep grazing across the blue pastures of sky, and silence so deep that you could hear a cricket chirp.

Today if you try to walk to work in New York City as I sometimes do, sirens split your eardrums, flashing lights dazzle your eyes, trucks roar and smoke like dragons, the air has a barely sublethal level of carbon-monoxide, the streets are paved with debris, and harried-looking people pour in and out of subway cars so begrimed and besmeared with graffiti that they resemble trolleys from hell.

Psychologically, the tension is increased by the stridency of the media and their preoccupation with gloom, doom, crime, disaster, murder, mayhem, flood, famine, pornography, perversion, inflation, taxation, and every other unpleasantness known to man.

In the olden days they used to say that bad coinage would drive out good, meaning that if inferior coins were circulated, people would hoard the good coins and refuse to spend them. This was known as Gresham's law. Well, there seems to be a kind of Gresham's law for the news media, in which bad news drives out good. If you don't believe me, go through your local newspaper sometime and hunt for good news. You'll see what I mean.

People set up defenses against this sort of environment as best they can. My dentist in New York, Dr. Arthur Merritt, is a wise man. He works hard, on his feet all day, the hum and roar of the great city just outside. But on the wall of his office he has hung a picture of an old covered bridge in Vermont, spanning a lovely rural stream where he used to swim as a boy. He can see it every time he looks up. It is so peaceful that it almost makes the patient feel peaceful—quite a trick when you are in a dentist's chair. It's a powerful aid to imaging, which is what it is meant to be.

Peace in a Tense Ball Game

Tension invades every area of our lives if we let it, even in athletics. Coaches are finding now that it is counterproductive, as they say, to scream at their players or exhort them to frenzied efforts. This is more likely to damage performance than improve it, because it heightens tension.

The great former Dodger baseball pitcher Carl Erskine is a good friend of ours. He told Ruth and me about a crucial game where he was the pitcher. It was the fifth of October, the fifth game of the series, the fifth inning, and it also happened to be Carl's fifth wedding anniversary. The Dodgers had a four-run lead when the Yankees came to bat. They put men on bases, brought in two men, and then, with two men still on base, someone hit a home run, bringing in a total of five runs within minutes, putting the Yankees one run ahead. Carl was in trouble.

The fans were howling vociferously, urging Charles Dressen, the Dodger manager, to remove Erskine and put in another pitcher. Erskine felt as if his nerves were stretched to the breaking point. His confidence in himself was being drained away by tension. It grew worse as he saw Charlie Dressen come out of the dugout and walk slowly to the mound.

Dressen held out his hand for the ball, Carl gave it to him. Seventy thousand fans watched breathlessly. Would Dressen summon a right-hander or another southpaw? Erskine waited. Dressen looked up reflectively at the sky. He asked mildly, "Isn't this your wedding anniversary, Carl?" Erskine nodded, astonished. "What are you doing tonight?" Dressen went on. "I hope you're taking Betty out to dinner." Erskine thought, *Seventy thousand fans watching me, and Charlie is asking about my wedding anniversary*! Dressen slapped the ball back into the pitcher's glove as he said, "You're my man, Carl. See if you can get the side out before dark." And he walked back to the dugout.

Thd Dodgers tied the score in the seventh inning and scored again in the top of the eleventh. Erskine got nineteen consecutive outs and the Dodgers won the game and eventually the series.

In another game, Carl told us, he felt his control slipping. The familiar, paralyzing tension began to build up in him. Tension is really a muscle spasm in the mind that can interfere with the smooth functioning of the muscles of the body. Carl knew he had to head it off somehow.

He backed off the mound, picked up the resin bag, flung it down. He turned his back on the plate, groping in his mind for something that would neutralize the tension. He prayed for help, and suddenly he remembered a trip he had taken some time before with another Dodger pitcher whose nickname was "Preacher" Roe. Carl and Preacher were out fishing when they heard, from across the lake, hymns being sung at a camp meeting.

As Carl stood beside the pitcher's box, he imaged that peaceful, pastoral scene and the words of one of those hymns came back into his mind:

> Drop Thy still dews of quietness,
> 'Til all our strivings cease;
> Take from our souls the strain and stress,
> And let our ordered lives confess
> The beauty of Thy peace.

Quietness. Peacefulness. Ordered lives. Beauty. The tranquil power in those words drove the tension out of Erskine's mind, and as soon as it was gone from his mind it was gone from his body. He turned back to the mound and began firing strikes past the batters.

Buried in a Thirty-Foot Snowdrift

There are, of course, crises much more crucial than a baseball game. But even when a situation seems hopeless, a calm, resolute imaging can hold off despair. Last winter I read a newspaper story about a truck driver in a midwestern state who was caught in a roaring blizzard. His wife had begged him not to make the run that night, for the radio was forecasting a snowstorm of major proportions. But he had a load of steel wire that had to be delivered, so he didn't listen to her. Halfway to his destination, the howling storm swept down on him. When driving conditions became impossible, he pulled the big truck off the road and went to sleep.

When he woke up, everything was dark. Although he didn't know it, the truck was buried in a snowdrift thirty feet deep. The truck was completely covered; no part of it was visible from the highway. The driver could not open the doors. He was trapped. On his CB radio, he could dimly hear the voices of state police and other rescue teams, but he could not communicate with them. His CB could receive but could not transmit through all the snow

For five days and nights he stayed in his icy tomb. He had no food. To quench his thirst he ate snow. Five days and nights. One hundred twenty endless hours. But he didn't panic. He didn't despair. He waited, calmly and stoically, to be rescued; and finally he was.

I was so impressed when I read his story that I called him on the telephone and told him how much I admired his courage and stamina. "Weren't you afraid?" I asked.

"No," he said. "I knew my brother would be looking for me. I knew he wouldn't rest until he found me. In my mind I could see him searching, searching all up and down that highway, never getting discouraged, never giving up. I could see him just as plain as day, finally locating the drift I was buried in. And as long as I could see him like that, I wasn't afraid. It was just a question of when he'd find me, not if he'd find me. And finally he did."

There was a classic use of imaging: a man in deep trouble vividly seeing a desired goal or outcome, holding it resolutely in his mind until it became a reality. He might have visualized himself starving, or frozen, or suffocated, but he didn't. He saw himself being rescued, and that image held the wolves of fear and panic at bay.

Among the useful imaging techniques for tension control that have come to my attention is a unique procedure outlined by Jo Kimmell in her book *Steps to Prayer Power*. She suggests a process of imaging in which one visualizes all the unhealthy mixture of thought which causes tension as flowing out of the body through the toes and fingers, until an emptying of stress is achieved.

The emptying procedure is followed by a refilling process in which a healthy mixture of thought, composed of serenity, wholeness, joy, and peace is imaged as being poured into the body to circulate throughout the entire being. The result is a feeling of relaxation and rest, a diminution of tension.

Let me end this chapter by giving you a remarkable example of the power of imaging, backed by faith. I came across it in a story I read recently by a North Carolina schoolteacher named Marilyn Ludolf. For almost sixteen years her life had been full of tension and misery because of an unsightly rash across her face. It ruined her appearance; it gave her terrible headaches; it made her desperately unhappy. Apparently nothing could be done about it. She consulted doctors and dermatologists; she tried every kind of lotion and skin preparation; she ate vitamins; she went on countless diets. Nothing helped.

Mrs. Ludolf was a Sunday-school teacher, and one day while she was teaching her class, the story flashed into her mind of the woman who touched the hem of Jesus' robe and was cured of a disease that, like her own, had plagued her for years. She realized suddenly that she had tried everything except turning to God, *really* turning to Him with faith that He could and would heal her.

So she decided to go into training, like an athlete, in an effort to strengthen her faith. She knew her faith needed strengthening because she hadn't been using it, and like an unused muscle it had become flabby and weak. She took a Bible with a concordance, and she looked up all the verses to be found under the headings of *healing*, *health*, and *faith*. She found thirty-five of them scattered throughout the Bible. She wrote them down, word for word "as sort of a training manual for my faith." (They are listed at the conclusion of this chapter.)

Then she began to carry these Scriptures everywhere she went. When her car stopped at a red light, at spare moments in the classroom, while doing housework, at night before falling asleep, she read the verses and meditated on them. This became her constant routine. And gradually the thirty-five passages slowly sank into the core of her being. She began to believe, really believe, that she could be healed.

Finally Mrs. Ludolf took a decisive leap of faith. She picked a certain day a few weeks away, and ringed it on the calendar. "Lord," she prayed, "this is the day I'm asking for complete healing."

Then she began one last exercise: visualizing her skin as clear and soft as a baby's. This was hard, because the terrible red rash and the painful headaches continued. "But after a while," she wrote, "this image, like the Scriptures, began to sink into the deep, believing places of my life." (There is a great phrase for you: "the deep, believing places of my life"— a poetic and accurate way of describing her subconscious mind.) She also began to thank the Lord fervently for healing her, although as yet there was no evidence that He had.

In the meantime, she kept on reading her dog-eared Scripture verses, although she had long since memorized them. Day after day went by. Day after day she meditated and affirmed and prayed. Gradually her rash began to fade and the painful headaches grew less frequent. And on the final day, the day she had marked on the calendar, she looked into the mirror through eyes brimming with tears, because the mirror told her that her affliction was gone.

"According to your faith be it unto you" (Matthew 9:29). Believe, pray, image, give thanks—and tension can be eliminated from your life.

Mrs. Ludolf did it.

You can do it, too.

Here are the thirty-five Scriptures Mrs. Ludolf used:

Proverbs 4:20–22	John 10:10
Romans 10:17	3 John 2
Matthew 7:7, 11	Hebrews 13:8
Matthew 8:7, 13	Malachi 4:2
Matthew 9:29, 35	Matthew 4:23, 24
Matthew 14:14	Psalms 91:9, 10
Matthew 15:30	Proverbs 3:7, 8
Matthew 17:20, 21	Exodus 15:26
Matthew 19:2	James 5:15
Mark 1:34	1 Peter 2:24
Mark 5:34	Psalms 42:11
Mark 10:52	Psalms 6:2
Mark 9:23	Psalms 41:4
Mark 11:22–24	Psalms 103:2, 3
Luke 6:19	Isaiah 53:4, 5
John 14:13, 14	Jeremiah 17:14
Acts 10:38	1 John 4:4
Galatians 3:13	

13
How to Deepen Your Faith

In the hundreds of letters that come to Ruth and me from people with problems, one of the most constant and recurring themes is lack of faith.

"I don't seem to have much faith," the unhappy refrain goes. "I try to believe, but my beliefs are shaky."

"Other people seem to have more faith than I do; what can I do to be like them?"

"Everybody tells me I should have faith, but nobody tells me how to acquire it."

"Why isn't my faith stronger? What can I do to deepen it?"

Month after month, year after year, the letters keep coming.

I sympathize with these seekers after faith, but really they are blocking themselves. When you *see* yourself as a person of inadequate faith, when you *accept* the idea that you are limited in this crucial area, when you *project* this image of yourself to others, you are really notifying your unconscious mind that you are the plaintive possessor of a permanent spiritual deficiency. If your unconscious mind accepts that image, as ultimately it will, it will program itself—and you—to perpetuate this unhappy state of affairs. That is why people tend to be, and to remain, what they keep telling themselves they are.

So the first thing the person who wishes to deepen his faith must do is change that negative image of himself as a faithless person to something else.

One way to accomplish this change is by using a powerful imaging technique that consists of just three words: *act as if*. So you think you don't have much faith? No matter: act as if you did. Act as if the whole of the gospel story, the good news proclaimed by Jesus that God loves us and cares for us, the marvelous promise He gave us that He would never abandon us, His assurance that we could have forgiveness of sins if we repented of them, His pledge that if we obeyed and believed we would have life eternal—act as if it were all true. Never mind if you feel it is too good to be true; never mind if your doubts seem overpowering; *act as if you believed*.

If you do, your unconscious mind will respond. It will say to itself, "Here is this person *acting* like a believer, so I am going to program him or her toward faith instead of away from it." And once your unconscious mind takes hold of that idea, you will find yourself being swept along by a current flowing ever more strongly from the arid deserts of doubt to the green fields of spiritual certainty.

Another thing: while you act as if, give thanks that this change in your life is actually taking place now. Even when you can't see it happening, even when you don't know for sure whether it is happening, give thanks, because the act of giving thanks for as-yet-unglimpsed benefits is in itself a powerful form of faith.

Great men have always known this. Someone once asked the famous composer Joseph Haydn how he managed to create such marvelous music. "When I decide to compose," he replied, "I pray and thank God that it has been accomplished. Then I do it. If it doesn't come the first time, I pray again. Then it comes!" There is a classic example of the prayerize-visualize-actualize sequence, strengthened and fortified by giving thanks in advance. Perhaps the event hasn't transpired yet, but the image of it exists in the mind of man and, when prayer is involved, in the timeless mind of God as well. Giving thanks under those circumstances is an expression of pure faith, and faith is the fuel in the tank of the invisible psychic engine that makes wonderful things happen.

Act as if was the favorite advice of an old friend of mine, Dr. Samuel M. Shoemaker. Whenever some skeptic asked him how to live a faith-filled life, that is what he urged them to do. Dr. Sam also had a technique called the "six *X*'s" that he liked to recommend. He said they made a very logical progression for the faith seeker, and they went like this:

> Exposure
> Explanation
> Experiment
> Experience
> Expression
> Expansion

The first step, *exposure*, is essential. How are you going to acquire faith, or deepen faith, unless you make contact with it, unless you go where it is?

This means going to church, because the atmosphere of a church, conditioned by prayer and sanctified by ceremony and ritual, is the place where faith is most likely to be found. The best place to know and understand a person is in that person's home. Likewise, it is easier and more natural to believe in God when you are in God's house. You have the reinforcement of other people's beliefs; your prayers mingle with their prayers. You have the conditioning of the surroundings: the architecture, the sacred music, the familiar passages from Scripture or prayer book, a whole backdrop that has evolved through the ages, all designed to direct and focus the mind on God. So if you want to strengthen your faith, you can hardly do without church attendance.

Another form of exposure is Bible reading; what better way to understand God than by reading His Word? Yet another form of exposure is associating with people who have a deep spiritual side to their nature, observing them, watching how faith illuminates their lives. Their faith may rub off on you! And nowadays there are lots of such people. You can find them everywhere, people who are enthusiastic believers.

Explanation comes next, because there are many aspects of religion that need explaining. The plan of salvation is a logical framework of thought so solid that it has survived for almost two thousand years, but much of it needs to be explained to the inquiring mind. Bible-study classes, small prayer groups, religious books and lectures, even sermons can be a part of this explaining process. And it is a process that never ends. Vast numbers of people are studying the Bible today, more than ever before, I'm sure.

You take the third step when you begin to *experiment* with what you have learned. Perhaps you start keeping a prayer diary, and look back after a month to see how many of your prayer requests have been answered. (You'll be astonished, I assure you!) Or perhaps you decide to experiment with tithing, or with forgiving someone who has wronged you. There are great spiritual benefits to be derived from these things, but you have to experiment with them before you can be convinced.

The fourth step comes when you actually begin to *experience* these benefits or perhaps when you have a life-changing spiritual encounter of some kind that would have been impossible without your growing faith.

The fifth stage comes when you feel ready and eager to give *expression* to your deepening convictions, witnessing to the power of Jesus Christ in your own personal experience and the joy that knowing Him has brought you.

And the sixth stage, as your spiritual growth continues, is where the love of God *expands* until it fills your whole consciousness and directs your whole life.

Dr. Sam's six-point formula has helped many people. Another powerful way to strengthen your faith is to image Jesus Christ coming into your life and dealing with some problem that may be troubling you as if it were actually, literally taking place.

Recently I read a book by a physician, Dr. David L. Messenger, titled *Dr. Messenger's Guide to Better Health*.

Dr. Messenger, a strong Christian, believes in what he calls "Wholistic Medicine," which means treating the patient as a whole—body, mind, and spirit, not just focusing on one set of symptoms or one particular complaint.

Before he attempts to treat the physical body, this brilliant doctor tries to locate areas of emotional hurt and relieve them. Dr. Messenger writes, in a vivid metaphor, that the octopus of anger and its internal tentacles of resentment, hatred, hostility, and bitterness have negative chemistry effects. In another place he tells us that people who "think well" tend to stay well, and people who "think sick" tend to get sick more often. I've been advocating these same ideas for years, so naturally I agree with Dr. Messenger. The Bible says it, too: "Heaviness [anxiety] in the heart of man maketh it stoop [weighs it down]" (Proverbs 12:25).

Your Greatest Hurt

But to get back to imaging: Dr. Messenger often asks a patient, "What is the biggest hurt that ever happened to you?" When he asked a woman patient that one day, she began to weep and told him that her biggest hurt was the constant bitter fighting and quarreling between her father and mother that finally resulted in her father's leaving home for good. She said the worst memory of all was of a scene where her mother became so enraged that she seized a butcher knife and tried to stab her father.

Dr. Messenger told the lady to relax, close her eyes, and visualize that scene again, just as it had happened twenty-five years earlier: the terrified child (herself), the enraged adults, the light gleaming on the deadly knife as her mother snatched it from the kitchen table. He urged her to relive all the painful emotions: the fear, the dread, the terror. Then he said to her, "Be aware of the presence of Jesus—the warm, loving, kind presence of the Person of Jesus. Now watch that scene and let Jesus do what He wants to do. When you're done, tell me about it."

After a few minutes, the woman opened her eyes and described how Jesus had walked over and gently taken the knife away from the mother. Then He had put His arms around both the mother and the father, and by the power of His infinite love had brought an end to their hatred and bitterness. Then He had picked the little girl (herself) up in His arms and had soothed and comforted her. And that simple but intense use of imaging, Dr. Messenger said, brought about a healing of the painful memories and was the first step in a physical healing for the patient as well.

That sort of imaging is close to prayer, and prayer itself is probably the surest and most direct way to strengthen your faith. If you meet someone who is attractive and appealing, and you want to know that person better, what do you do? You talk to him or her, don't you? You try to communicate. You offer yourself in what you hope will be an ever-increasing exchange of ideas and affection and intimacy. Well, that is exactly what prayer is—an exchange between you and the great Father that created all life, including yours. It is awe inspiring and almost incredible that this vast Being, this infinite Power, is available for such an exchange. But He is. That is the marvelous truth, the good news of the Gospel, the message that Jesus Christ Himself brought to us.

If you doubt that truth, you are opening the door to negative imaging. If you say to yourself, "Well, I'm not all that sure there is a God, or even if there is, I don't feel any certainty that I can communicate with Him," then you are letting doubt triumph over faith, and this uncertainty will run like jangling discord through all the major areas of your life.

If you let doubt become dominant, you probably won't even try to pray, and when you don't pray you are cutting yourself off from a tremendous source of peace and power. I know about this from firsthand experience, because I try to talk to the Lord all through the day. Nothing very formal or fancy. I just talk to Him as I would to a dearly loved friend who is always by my side. This is as close as I can get to the biblical injunction to "pray without ceasing" (1 Thessalonians 5:17). That injunction, of course, is hard to carry out in our busy, fragmented lives. But when you do find time to pray for any sustained length of time, remarkable things happen, especially when your prayers are directed toward the needs of others, not your own needs.

Wide Awake at 3:00 A.M.

Not long ago, for example, I woke up at 3:00 A.M. on a Sunday morning. I had gone to bed early, as I always do on a Saturday night when I have to preach the next day, but here I was, all of a sudden, wide-awake. I tried every known device to go back to sleep. I said the Twenty-third Psalm half a dozen times. I counted sheep (a pretty weak form of imaging, I'll admit!). But still I could not get back to sleep. Finally I got up at four o'clock, went into my library, and picked up one book and magazine after another. Nothing held my interest.

Some years ago in Switzerland, I purchased a large and beautiful eagle carved from a single block of wood, and brought it back to my library. Made by one of the old-time Swiss wood-carvers, it is really a work of art. The eagle has his wings spread and is taking off from some high eminence. I sat looking at the eagle and remembering when I bought it, and the old man who made it, and then, naturally, I began to say aloud a passage of Scripture: ". . . they shall mount up with wings as eagles; they shall run, and not be weary; and they shall walk, and not faint" (Isaiah 40:31).

This in turn led to a thought about a friend, a pastor who says that occasionally, when he needs spiritual help, he goes into the church and walks the aisles. He places his hand on the pew where a certain person sits and prays for that person by name. And he repeats the process at various pews in the empty church. The pastor says that this procedure always brings great blessing to him as well as to the persons he prays for. So, motivated by my friend's example, there alone in the early morning, I started to visualize everyone I should pray for.

The first person was my wife, Ruth. Then I prayed for our three children and their spouses, then for our eight grandchildren. I prayed for all the relatives I could call to mind. Then my mind went to the church and I prayed for the other ministers. I prayed for all the secretaries. Then one by one I prayed for all the elders and all the deacons. Finally I began to visualize the congregation at the church and prayed for everyone I could think of by name. Then I prayed for the doormen in our apartment house and for all the people with whom I am associated in any way.

Actually, I must have prayed for five hundred people by name. By this time it was 6:00 A.M. All of a sudden I felt better than I had felt in a long time. I was full of energy, and boundless enthusiasm surged within me. I wouldn't have gone back to sleep for anything. I was ravenously hungry and went and awakened my wife.

"Get up! It's 6:00 A.M.," I said. "I'm hungry and let us have no piddling breakfast. I want bacon and eggs, the whole works!" And I ate a big, man-sized breakfast.

I went to the church and delivered a sermon and shook hands with hundreds of people. Then I went to a luncheon and gave a talk, and on to an afternoon engagement, and at eleven o'clock that night I was still going strong. I was not even tired! Such an excess of energy was mine as to astound me, and with it came a tremendous new feeling of love for life.

Now, I'm not psychologist enough to explain exactly what happened. I guess I got outside myself. Consciously, even subconsciously, I completely forgot myself in loving all those other people and praying for them and taking their burdens on myself. But this didn't add any weight, either. It added wings! And it left me happy and joyous, revitalized, reborn. Actually, I rose up "with wings as eagles."

So now, whenever I feel enervated or depressed, I repeat that prayer process. And I offer this experience as a suggestion of how you, too, may not only help others by prayer but also find marvelous new life for yourself.

Prayer has always been the most effective way to get close to the Lord. Sometimes when Ruth and I are in England, in the Lake District, we return to the place where Wordsworth is said to have written his poem "The Daffodils." Wordsworth tells us that in such spots it was his custom to imagine (image) Jesus as actually being close beside him. He would quote some words of the Savior, then reflectively say, "I wonder what the tone of Jesus' voice was when He said that?" He would "listen" to what the voice might have sounded like—the tonal quality, the depth of feeling. And then he would ask, "I wonder what the expression on His face was like when He said those words?" By imaging Jesus so vividly, lovingly filling in all those details, the poet felt the reality of His actual presence.

Nothing is more faith strengthening than to pray and have your prayer answered. In our counseling work, Ruth and I have learned, when a human problem is brought to us, to put it into a spiritual dimension by praying about it. Once that is done with sincerity and humility, we often find that mighty forces come to our aid.

God's Guidance Always Works

One time, for example, we found ourselves involved in one of those difficult human problems that arise when a person with excellent qualifications and abilities just doesn't happen to fit into the particular niche where he finds himself. In this case, it was a young minister of splendid character and great talent with a most attractive family, who had joined the staff of a church. But things had not worked out as hoped. He was greatly troubled as we, his friends, were about where he would go and what he would do.

In one discussion, the young minister said a bit disconsolately that an ambition he and his attractive wife had had for years now seemed more remote than ever. When pressed to reveal what this was, he said that he had always dreamed of starting a religious community in the mountains, a kind of retreat where young skiers might be attracted in winter and summer tourists might come in warm weather. He even knew of such a place that had a rustic building the owner might be persuaded to sell. "But of course," he said, "that is just a dream. Maybe in five years. . . ." His voice trailed off dejectedly.

Ruth had been praying hard for a solution for this young couple, and she kept turning over their dream in her mind.

Finally she said to them, "Why wait five years? Why don't you try to get started on it now?"

"We'd love to," they said. "But we don't have the money. It's as simple as that."

We all nodded gloomily. No money. Too bad.

But the Lord had heard Ruth's prayers, and He was not going to let us get away with this negative, downbeat attitude. So in the middle of the night He put into Ruth's head an idea so simple and startling that she sat up in bed and began to shake me. "Norman," she said, "wake up! I've got an idea!"

"Can't it wait till morning?" I mumbled.

"No, it can't! You know those books of yours that were sold through *Guideposts*, the ones you can't accept any royalties from because you're the president of a nonprofit organization?"

"Ruth," I moaned, "are you waking me up in the middle of the night just to remind me of money that I've earned and can't have?"

"That's right," she said. "The money is there, and you can't have it for yourself. We have been holding it to donate to some worthwhile cause. Why don't we use that money to help our friends buy that building and start living their dream now?"

It was amazing how the Lord worked things out. The building has been converted into the religious center that the young couple had dreamed of for so long.

The moral seems clear: When you put an apparently unsolvable problem into the spiritual dimension by praying about it, watch out—because things are going to start happening! Good things. Abundant things. Astonishing things. What you image can really happen.

Sometimes, I think, people refuse to believe that prayer brings such quick solutions. They say, "Oh, that's just coincidence!" or "Oh, well, that would probably have happened anyway." This is negative imaging that can only serve to dilute what little faith the person may have to begin with.

But sometimes the cause and effect of prayer is so quick and so powerful that it converts a person into a total believer for the rest of his life. Not long ago I was in a taxi and noticed that the driver had a Dutch-sounding name. When I asked him about it, he said that he was indeed from Rotterdam. So I told him that I was a minister of the church which the Dutch established in New York way back in 1628, and we had a friendly chat.

As we drove along he asked, "Have you time to let me tell you a little story? It is about the first time I really met God, and it shows how good God is. I have great faith, sir, and I know that I can never get outside the care and love of God.

"It was close to the end of World War II. I was a little boy in Holland. Our country had been ravaged. The Germans had been driven out, but we were left absolutely destitute. We had ration stamps, but they weren't any good, for we had no food at all. There was no food in the warehouses or in the stores or in the country districts. Holland had been swept clean. There was nothing left.

"We were reduced to eating beets out of the fields and it was a kind of beet that is dangerous to eat without long cooking—and even then, if you don't accompany it with other food, a chemical reaction will bloat and distend the stomach. Some people died from that chemical reaction." He shook his head and was silent for a moment. Then he continued, "You know how beautiful Holland tulips are? We dug the bulbs out of the ground and ate them. That was all we had. We were desperate."

Again he was silent. I could tell he was deeply moved by those memories. Finally he went on. "A notice from our pastor went around, telling us that there would be a meeting in the church. He said that since there was no other hope, we would have a meeting and pray to God and tell Him we were His children and ask Him to feed us. It was the only thing we could do. The big church was packed; two thousand people were present. There was no sermon. We just prayed, hour after hour. The pastor prayed. People prayed aloud all over the church. We sat their huddled together, praying to God.

"I was only a little boy, but all of a sudden I became aware that God was right there with us. His presence was so strong that I was almost frightened. I could feel Him in my heart. I knew that He was there and I knew that somehow He was going to take care of us poor, starving people.

"Then we sang out one of those great old Dutch hymns of faith and we went out to the streets and to our homes. With gnawing, empty stomach I went to bed and fell asleep. Early the next morning we were awakened by the roar of a tremendous armada of allied airplanes over Rotterdam, and there began an unbelievable shower of food. The sky was full of big packages, dangling from parachutes, that came floating down to the streets of Rotterdam, filling the avenues with good food. And we ate. And we were saved."

He glanced back at me from the driver's seat as he said, "As long as I live, I will believe that God heard those prayers and out of His big heart of love He fed His children."

I do believe it. And I am sure you do, also. How could anyone doubt a soul-stirring story like that? Why try to analyze it or question it or explain it away? Why not let it move you and strengthen your faith?

And be thankful.

14
Imaging in Everyday Life

So far in this book, imaging has been presented as a powerful device to achieve major goals and objectives. And so it is. But imaging can be used in many lesser ways to smooth out the minor wrinkles of living. For example, my friend Dr. Charles L. Allen, the popular minister-writer, tells a story in his book *Perfect Peace* about a woman who suffered from insomnia. Nothing very unusual about that. But her solution to the problem was interesting. She was a lover of flowers, and a skilled arranger of them. And so, when sleep didn't come easily, lying there in the dark she would visualize a table with a handsome flower vase on it and two dozen long-stemmed roses lying beside it. She would hold the scene in her mind until it became almost real: the rich grain of the wood in the tabletop, the flowing curves of the vase, the pale green rose stems, the ruby petals glowing with velvety color.

Then she would see herself slowly picking up the roses, one by one, and arranging them in the vase. First she would visualize the vase with one tall flower, then two, then three— each carefully placed for artistic effect. Each time she added a flower, she would move back a few paces and study the composition. And according to Charles Allen, she never was able to complete the arrangement with all twenty-four flowers, because she always fell asleep!

Suppose you would like to redecorate a room in your house, or buy new furniture for the patio. Suppose, as is so often the case, you don't think you can afford to do it right away. What is to prevent you from imaging that room or that patio just the way you would like to have it? Fill in all the details—the color of the curtains, the pattern of the carpet, the kind of mirror you want above the mantelpiece— see it all in your mind's eye. It is a lot of fun, it doesn't cost a thing, and the more vivid the image, the better chance that someday it will become a reality.

When James Whistler, the great American painter, was first married, he and his wife were so poor that the only furniture they had was a bed. But this did not discourage them. In every empty room of their modest house they sketched with chalk, on the floor, the outline of each piece of additional furniture that they intended to have someday. Inside the outline they added a detailed description of what it would look like. They imaged their dream house furnished just as they wanted it to be. And the time came when that vision became a happy reality. Why? Because they pushed beyond the fuzzy, indistinct yearnings that many people settle for and *focused* their wishes with great intensity of imaging. Those chalk marks and detailed descriptions on the floor gave a substance and a reality to the dream that otherwise it would never have had. And their unconscious minds went to work instantly, providing the energy and the drive and the confidence that the young couple needed to reach their goal.

Suppose you would like to travel. Do you want to visit England or Italy, or see the Grand Canyon, or go flying down to Rio? Don't just sit and vaguely wish. Go to a travel bureau. Get some brochures. Better still, get some maps and trace the route you would like to follow. Go to the library and take out some history books. Learn all you can about the place you want to visit, its history, the people who are living there. Then image yourself against that background.

If your dream is visiting the Holy Land, visualize yourself standing in Bethany at the spot where Jesus raised Lazarus from the dead. See yourself on the shores of Galilee where He commanded the wind and the waves to be still.

Tell yourself that the same waves and the same wind are still there, waiting for you to visit them. Imagine yourself in Jerusalem, putting your hand on the olive trees in the Garden of Gethsemane or at the tomb where the stone was rolled away. Don't let negative considerations like lack of money creep in, because your unconscious mind will seize upon a negative signal just as readily as it will react to a positive one.

Does this kind of dreaming, which is just another form of imaging, guarantee that someday you will find yourself in Rio or in the Holy Land or in England or Italy? No, it doesn't: life doesn't hand out ironclad guarantees. But it raises the probabilities so enormously that it is foolish not to take advantage of it.

The thing to remember is that an image vividly conceived and stubbornly held has a reality of its own. Once a young man spoke to me after I had made a speech in Los Angeles on the subject of positive thinking. He had a dream of going into electronics, building a small factory, and he described it in detail. He had it all worked out in his mind. "But," he said, "I don't have capital and I don't have any credit. I don't know if I will ever get it built."

"But it is built," I told him. "You have already created this factory. It exists—in your mind."

"It is just a vision," he said, "just a dream."

"That's great," I said. "That is the first step and the most important step. Never tell yourself that your factory doesn't exist, because it does. You have already built it. It is there, imaged in your consciousness. The next step is to get it out of your head and onto a piece of ground somewhere. And you'll take that second step as surely as you took the first. It is just a matter of patience and persistence and determination and time."

First Built by Imaging

"You mean it's built?" he said incredulously. "You mean I have already built it? Gosh, that is an exciting idea!"

"First the dream," I told him. "The dream or image worked out in detail. The image so vivid that you can see it like a three-dimensional picture glowing in your mind. Then the hard work and the discipline and the willingness to take risks and the refusal to let go of the dream or let it fade. Put those elements together and you can't miss. You can't fail. You'll see."

He went away, and I suppose I really never expected to see him again. But about a year later, when I was greeting people after a service at Marble Collegiate Church in New York, he came along in the line. "Remember me?" he said. "Just wanted to say two words to you. It's built!"

"Wonderful!" I said to him. "But remember, it was built all the time!"

Great athletes use imaging constantly, sometimes consciously, sometimes without being fully aware of what they are doing. Have you ever watched a champion high jumper just before he makes his jump? Usually he stares at the ground for a long moment before he begins his run. And in that moment he is visualizing himself sailing across the bar. He is flinging his image over the bar, you might say, and if his body fully accepts that image, it is probably going to follow.

Years ago I heard a story about Jim Thorpe, the great American-Indian athlete whose legendary feats in sports are still revered and remembered. With the rest of the American team, Thorpe was on his way to Europe by ship to compete in the Olympic Games. Each day the athletes would work out on the ship's deck, some running, some jumping, some lifting weights. The scene was one of furious activity. One of the coaches was astonished, therefore, to come upon Thorpe one day sitting on the deck, leaning back against a lifeboat, eyes closed, not even in his track suit.

"Thorpe," the coach said sharply, "what do you think you're doing?"

The big, bronzed athlete opened one eye. "I'm watching myself win the decathalon," he said. And closed it again.

Imaging. Thorpe had never heard of the word, but he had adopted the technique and he knew it was more valuable than any amount of mere physical preparation. He was seeing himself win the decathalon *in advance*. And when the event finally took place, the image became the reality.

Well, you may say, suppose two or three other athletes from England or France or Germany had employed the same technique—what then? In that case, I would say, the contestant with the greatest physical endowments and the most vivid image of himself being victorious would win the event. But if the physical endowments were equal, then the owner of the strongest will to win, as reflected in that self-image of being the winner, would come away with the prize.

My friend W. Clement Stone, a well-known Chicago insurance man, founded a magazine called *Success Unlimited*. Not long ago it carried a fascinating article about a young graduate student named Steve DeVore. Steve, a psychology student, was reading a textbook on biofeedback one wintry afternoon and at times idly watching a TV program about championship bowling. Steve was an occasional bowler whose highest score was an unspectacular 163. But now, watching the champion bowlers reel off strings of strikes, he began to wonder if he might not somehow use the images on the TV screen to program his own mind and possibly increase his bowling skills.

So, blocking out all other thoughts and making himself as relaxed as possible, he tried to impress on his memory the images of the top bowlers making their very high scores. When the program ended, he played the images back in his mind, just as if he had a video tape inside his head. Finally, still concentrating intensely, he want out to a nearby bowling alley. There again he replayed his mental tape, telling his mind to direct and control his body and telling his body to become an instrument of his mind.

Steve DeVore then proceeded to bowl an unheard-of nine strikes in a row for a score of 286 out of a possible 300.

In his second game he bowled seven strikes. Then his concentration faltered, and his game began to slide downhill. But DeVore was so impressed with what imaging could do that he started his own company, called Sybervision, to market a system of thought to athletic teams and individuals. The results, according to some professional coaches who have tried it, are nothing short of amazing.

Imaging can reach far beyond sports into almost every aspect of daily life. Suppose you are carrying a burden of guilt for some past mistake or transgression. Suppose you have tried the time-tested remedies — ackknowledging your fault, making restitution, asking God to forgive you — and still feel unworthy and troubled. This load of unresolved guilt is draining strength and purpose from you. Can imaging help?

Perhaps it can. Try visualizing a blackboard with a jumble of disconnected words and phrases, or a tangle of scrawled mathematical problems with wrong answers — in short, a sorry record of mistakes. Then image a shining figure, the Lord Himself, sweeping a sponge or a damp cloth across that blackboard, wiping it clean, preparing it for another, stronger, better effort. The Lord has forgiven your sins and mistakes. Then forgive yourself, for if you don't, the old guilt circle will repeat itself. Run this total picture sequence over and over in your mind. What you are imaging is forgiveness and acceptance, and if the vision is vivid enough, a great sense of peace and well-being will follow.

Suppose you are a victim of depression. Picture that doleful word spelled out in a gigantic electric sign on a mountaintop, with letters ten feet tall. It can be seen at night for miles. Then image the first two and the eighth letters suddenly extinguished. What's left? Two positive and vigorous words: *press on*!

Picture Yourself as Confident

Are you facing some challenge in your job where you doubt your ability to cope? Image yourself meeting the challenge, solving the problem — and give thanks for that solution in advance. Picture yourself filled with a surge of confidence and energy that sweeps away doubts and fears. Image your mind coming alive with fresh, new energy, crackling with new concepts, teeming with new ideas.

If you paint these images vividly enough, they may affect not only you but also the person or persons you are dealing with. In Australia a couple of years ago, Ruth and I met a dynamic and attractive woman named Lorraine St. Clair. She was the Australian representative for a company that specialized in reproductions of antique jewelry. Lorraine had conceived the idea of displaying these items in a real antique breakfront where prospective customers could look through the glass and see pieces of jewelry on black or red velvet—the effect was stunning.

Later Lorraine came to visit us in New York. She was very interested in our church and in the way we lived our lives. She said she had no spiritual training herself, and she wanted to find out more about such things. Ruth told her about tithing and the spiritual rewards it brings; this seemed to fascinate Lorraine and she became a tither herself.

She told us that her company wanted her to go to Europe and try to establish a market there for the jewelry. She had no connections or contacts there, but someone had told her that if she could persuade one of the principal stores to take this merchandise, others would follow.

So Lorraine fixed this goal in her mind. She began to image herself meeting the key marketing people and persuading them to carry the line of jewelry. She focused on this vision with great intensity before she left Australia and while she was flying to Europe.

Upon arriving, she called a man who was a chief buyer for a well-known store. She told him that she had studied his merchandising techniques (this was true) and admired them very much. She also told him about herself and said that she had a line of jewelry that she hoped to establish. To her amazement, the man said that he would see her. Result? Just as she had imaged it. Instant success.

Now how often would the chief buyer from a great store respond to an unknown vendor of jewelry and look at her samples? Not very often. But Lorraine had imaged precisely that outcome. Had something reached out and influenced the man on the other end of the telephone wire? Again, who can say?

Imaging can help in many other ways. Suppose you are torn with grief because a loved one has died. Surely it helps to image or visualize a future reunion with that person in the "land that is fairer than day." If the person was old or frail or feeble, picture him as vigorous and vital, as he was in the prime of life. Image the wonderful conversations and activities you will share when you are with him once again. Picture his eyes full of joy and happiness because he is reunited with you—forever.

Once or twice I have had a vision of my father and later one of my brother, Bob, after they had left this earthly life. In both instances, they looked vibrant and youthful and happy. They seemed to know that I could see them, too, because they raised their hands in the old familiar gesture of greeting and affection as if to say, "Don't worry about us. Everything is all right. We'll see you later." Those experiences, I think, were a form of imaging carried one step further into a reality we are seldom allowed to glimpse. But that reality is eternally there.

Image of a Country Home

There are other areas of imaging where things happen that are equally hard to understand. You may recall the clairvoyant vision of Mary Crowe that I described in the first chapter of this book. Something similar happened years ago to some good friends of mine, Dr. William S. Bainbridge and his mother. Dr. Bainbridge's mother, a widow, grew tired of life in New York City and decided she wanted a place in the country. She had very definite ideas about the kind of place she wanted. She said she could visualize it clearly in her mind, right down to the last detail. But she and her son were unable to find one that suited her or that was like the place she imaged.

Finally they started praying about the problem, reading the Bible and asking for guidance. Meanwhile, the image in Mrs. Bainbridge's mind remained as clear as ever. As she was reading Scripture one day, a certain passage seemed to leap out at her: "And let us arise, and go up to Bethel . . ." (Genesis 35:3). She felt that it had great significance for her. Her son could think of no place in the New York area called Bethel, but Mrs. Bainbridge said there must be one. Furthermore, she felt a strange conviction that the house she was seeking was there.

Finally they discovered that there was indeed a town named Bethel in Connecticut, near Danbury. But when they drove up there and Mrs. Bainbridge described her dream house to a realtor, he shook his head. "There's no place like that around here that I know of," he said.

"It's got to be here," Mrs. Bainbridge insisted.

The realtor was sympathetic but firm: there was no such house in Bethel. So the Bainbridges went back to New York.

Three days later the realtor called them. "I was wrong," he said sheepishly. "There is such a house after all, just as you described it, that I wasn't aware of. But it is not for sale."

Back went the Bainbridges to Bethel. When they saw the house, they were astounded; it matched Mrs. Bainbridge's image exactly. Furthermore, the owners said that within the past forty-eight hours a sudden change of jobs had made it necessary for them to leave town. Mrs. Bainbridge bought the house and lived in it happily for many years.

"And let us arise, and go up to Bethel." Was it all just coincidence? Who can say?

One thing seems certain: The mind has unexplored powers, and most of the time such powers remain unused. In our day-to-day activities, we are not using more than a fraction of our brain capacity. I have experienced this extra and normally unused power of the mind on various occasions myself.

One night in a southern city, for example, I was getting ready to make a speech and needed a certain person's name. I just couldn't remember it. I looked through all my papers and couldn't find it. I was to go onstage in five minutes. I had to have this name, or at least I thought I did. I remembered that some psychiatrist had said that if you relax and call upon your deeper mind, which never forgets anything, your deeper mind will deliver what you need.

It so happened that this talk was being given in a theater, and I had noticed an old rocking chair behind the curtain. I asked the chairman about the program and he said, "A lady is going to sing two songs before you are introduced."

"Have her sing three," I said. "I am going around behind the curtain and sit in that old rocking chair."

So I went around back and sat in the rocking chair. "Now," I said, addressing my subconscious mind, "I understand that you never forget anything, and everything I ever did, thought, read or heard is stored down inside of you somewhere. I need this name. I know there is greater capacity in you than I normally use, and I have not called on you very often for a special favor. But now, subconscious mind, I want this piece of information and I want it right away. I've got to have it and I believe you are going to deliver it to me."

After I said that, I sat back and relaxed. I could literally feel the subconscious mind down inside of myself going into high gear. I could almost hear the wheels spinning around. And when I came out from around the curtain, the name popped up like toast from the toaster. I went out on the platform and tried to tell my subconscious mind to deliver me some more material, but that was all it would give me that evening.

What a strange tapestry this imaging is! So many patterns. So many threads. All interconnected in ways that sometimes seem to defy logical interpretation. But I am convinced that the basic premise is true: as Emerson said, "The soul contains the event that shall befall it."

Which is just another way of saying that if you image something strongly enough, you help to make that something happen. Imaging *does* affect future events. But the decision to do the imaging is yours.

Finally, may I point out that imaging has its own formula: 1) the goal, 2) the purpose, 3) prayer activity, 4) thoughtful planning, 4) innovative thinking, 6) enthusiasm, 7) organized hard work, and 8) always holding the image of success firmly in mind. If this formula is faithfully carried out, the desired results will be achieved despite all difficulties or setbacks.

I was asked to be the speaker at a big rally in Columbus, Ohio, on behalf of World Neighbors, a service organization engaged in helping deprived people abroad. The meeting was organized and directed by Dr. Roy Burkhardt, an enthusiastic, dedicated, and able leader. He was also a confirmed positive thinker.

When I arrived at the Columbus airport at three o'clock in the afternoon, it was in an almost torrential rainstorm accompanied by high winds that drove the rain in sheets. But there to welcome me with a big smile was Roy. "The hall is full!" he cried. "The hall is full!"

Mystified, I replied, "Why Roy, it is only 3:00 P.M. and the meeting is scheduled for 8:00 P.M. Certainly the hall cannot be filled five hours ahead of time."

"Oh, yes, the hall is full," he insisted. Then it dawned upon me. He was visualizing the hall as full. He was imaging it packed to capacity, and it was a large auditorium at that.

He took me to the hotel and the rain continued in a drenching downpour all afternoon and evening. Finally at eight o'clock, when Roy and I and ex-governor John W. Bricker walked onto the stage, that big hall was indeed full and people were standing.

What accounted for that packed house? The imaging formula is the answer. A goal, a purpose, lots of prayer, planning, thinking, enthusiasm, organization, and always intense, continuous imaging. This overcame every adverse condition, including one of the worst rainstorms I have ever experienced.

"The hall is full." Life is full, also, and always will be if you so image it and forever keep God in it.

15
The Imaging Process in Making and Keeping Friends

How do you conduct your life so that people are drawn to you? How do you get people to have a favorable attitude toward you? How do you persuade people to love you or—perhaps just as important—like you?

These are important questions for every one of us. William James, the great psychologist, said that one of the deepest drives in human nature is the desire to be appreciated, which is just another way of saying that everyone wants to be liked.

We all have this desire, and yet you know as well as I do that some people have more success in this area than others. These people seem to win friends easily and readily. They are popular. They are considered attractive, or charming, or helpful, or likable. People in trouble turn to them. Even their in-laws like them!

But there are other individuals who are not like that. Something seems to block them off from other people—and other people from them. They don't attract; they repel.

And this is often a sad and painful thing, because they feel isolated and friendless without quite knowing why.

I was giving a talk not long ago at a convention of men who were executives in the automotive industry. At the luncheon preceding my speech, I was seated at a table with several men. One was a man of considerable intellectual brilliance. His mind was sharp and perceptive, his conversation incisive and stimulating. Yet there was a certain something that kept me from really being drawn to him.

Later I asked one of his associates about him. "Poor Bill," the associate said. "He is without question one of the most able men I've ever done business with. But not long ago he came to me and said, 'Charlie, would you please tell me something? Why is it people don't like me? I seem to get just so close to them and then a barrier goes up that I cannot penetrate. What is the trouble?'"

"And what did you tell him?" I asked.

He was silent for a moment. "I really didn't tell him anything," he said at last, "because I didn't know how. But did you happen to notice those two scholastic-achievement keys hanging from his watch chain? I think somehow, unconsciously perhaps, Bill projects the impression that he considers himself superior to the person he's dealing with. It is a very subtle thing, but it is there. Instead of saying, 'I care about you,' something in his manner says, 'I think I'm a little smarter than you.' And maybe he is. But all the same, it turns people off."

"You should have told him what you just told me," I commented. "You would have been doing him a favor. He might have put those academic keys away and started projecting a different image. So if you ever get another opening. . . ."

"You're right," he said thoughtfully. "I will keep it in mind."

Suppose you feel that someone dislikes you and that therefore you have grounds for disliking him—what should you do about it?

The first and most advisable thing to do is take a long, dispassionate look at yourself. Two thousand years ago, Jesus Christ put the essence of the whole thing into one short sentence: You must love your neighbor as yourself. Are you hypersensitive, suspicious, quarrelsome, wary, hostile, aggressive, contentious? You will never like your neighbor, because you don't like yourself. Are you quick-tempered, jealous, demanding, complaining? Same problem. If you want to associate on a good, friendly, normal, creative level with other people, you have to do a job on yourself—until you like yourself.

Imaging can help, because you can zero in on a character flaw and then picture yourself acting in the opposite manner. Take anger, for example—an extremely unpleasant characteristic, almost guaranteed to cause you to lose friends and make enemies. Suppose you know you have a quick temper—a short fuse, as they say. When something ignites it, hold a picture in your mind of yourself calmly extinguishing it. Or if you can't completely extinguish it, at least delay it. Very often the best cure for anger is delay.

Some years ago, I was asked to serve on a committee that was set up to study ways in which religious organizations could further the cause of world peace. A meeting was held, and it was certainly the most unpeaceful committee meeting I have ever attended. Several of the members had very firm ideas about the subject of peace, and if those ideas weren't accepted, they got very hostile about it. It became a superheated meeting. Voices were raised. Tables were pounded. Then one man rose and, with an air of great deliberation, took off his jacket, undid his tie, and lay down on a couch that was there in the office. Discussion ceased abruptly as we all stared at the man. Somebody asked, "What's the matter? Aren't you feeling well?"

"I'm feeling fine," the man said. "I just noticed I was getting mad, that's all. And I have found that it is difficult to get mad lying down." He went on to give a little lecture on how keeping the body relaxed keeps emotions under control. He spoke in a very low voice.

"Speak up!" somebody said. "We can't hear what you are saying."

"That is the trouble with this meeting," the man on the couch said. "Too much speaking up too loudly. You can't argue in a whisper." Then he drew attention to his hands, which were resting limply with fingers spread and relaxed. He said, "I've noticed that when I get mad my fingers get tense, and before you know it I've clenched my fist. So I picture myself like this, with my fingers uncurled. With my fingers relaxed, it is very hard to get mad."

Well, I never did forget that man. He imaged himself out of a state of hostility and aggressiveness, and he carried the rest of us right along with him.

Another unlovely and unlovable quality is irritability, which often seems to be a combination of exasperation and impatience. The other day, while waiting to make a telephone call in a crowded airport where all the phones were in use, I noticed a distinguished-looking, silver-haired man in one of the booths, trying to put through a call. He got a busy signal half a dozen times. And what did this great executive do? He slammed the phone down so hard that it bounced off the hook and ricocheted around the booth on the end of its wire, an exhibition of plain, unadulterated infantilism.

We're all subject to exasperating happenings, from a broken shoelace to a friend who forgets a lunch date with you. There is a text, the twenty-first chapter of Luke, verse nineteen, that I like to repeat to myself under such circumstances: "In your patience possess ye your souls." If you practice spiritual patience you can rise above these inevitable annoyances. You can block them out, bring them under mental control. You have to decide who is going to call the shots: you or the annoyance. Patience through prayer and a quiet attitude is the best way.

When Someone Rubs You the Wrong Way

What if some person rubs you the wrong way? Here again, it is possible to learn to have an objective, scientific, dispassionate attitude. If you practice the two principles of spiritual patience and objective observation when someone does something to annoy you, you are not going to become irritated or angry. You are going to react as a scientist. A scientist is an objective, disciplined person who wants to know the causes behind circumstances. He reacts dispassionately, that is, without heat. So, acting as a scientific observer of the person whose actions annoy you, you will say to yourself, "I wonder what emotional conflict he has? What trouble is there in his life? Is he driven by some frustration or defeat?" Your reaction will be scientific and objective rather than emotional. You may even find yourself trying to help him solve his problem instead of resenting him.

I'll admit this requires greatness of spirit, because the natural tendency is to hit back. But it is a wonderfully satisfying experience when you have learned to study another person objectively and thereby avoid personal resentment.

Suppose you're having a disagreement with your wife, as we all do from time to time. Suppose she is being a real problem, or so you think. Try sitting and looking at her in a calm and pensive manner. This may be difficult, because if she is very annoyed with you she will say, "Why are you looking at me that way?"

"I'm studying you," you will say. "You used to be the greatest, sweetest girl. You were always so kind to me, and I loved you for it. Now you are upset and irritable, and I'm wondering why. Maybe it is my fault. Perhaps I'm just no good."

Do you know what she will do? She will start to defend you against yourself. "You're all right and I love you," she will firmly declare.

So there you are; the situation has been eased. You have dealt with her on a basis of spiritual psychology instead of simply reacting emotionally to her emotional state.

You will find that this principle holds true in dealing with your children, your business associates, and your friends in general. "I will study this person objectively," you say to yourself when conflicts or difficulties arise. "He has a soul, so I will treat him spiritually." You can get along with almost anybody, peacefully and without irritation, if you will refuse to be hurt and if you will look at the other person from a dispassionate and scientific point of view.

A visitor once asked Robert E. Lee, the great Confederate leader, what he thought of a certain individual.

"I think he is a very fine gentleman," Lee replied.

"He goes around saying some very uncomplimentary things about you," the visitor told the general. "What do you think of that?"

"You didn't ask me what he thought of me," Lee replied calmly. "You asked me what I thought of him."

The great general was too big to stoop to pettiness. That is why even his adversaries admired and respected him.

"Love your enemies . . ." Jesus Christ told us. ". . . bless them . . . pray for them . . ." (Matthew 5:44). It sounds hard. It is hard. But if you can bring yourself to do it, it will banish hate and anger from your heart and often turn an enemy into a friend. Christ is really telling us to let go of ill will, to image a reconciliation taking place. If you can force yourself to do this, the rewards are very great.

I remember a big, rough, tough, aggressive businessman who came to me after church services one day and said he wanted to acquire the spiritual power I had been preaching about. It sounded good to him. How could he get it? I listed the conventional answers to such questions and he went away, saying he would do as I suggested.

But a few weeks later he reappeared, saying that nothing worked. He prayed, he had read the Bible, he had cleaned up some dubious areas of his life, but he still had no feeling of spiritual power and he wanted to know what was wrong.

This time I talked to him in depth, and gradually it became apparent that his mind was full of hate and resentment for some of his business competitors. He was a big man and it was a big hatred. As a spiritual doctor I knew what he had to do if he wanted to have the power he was seeking, but I also knew that he was going to balk at the prescription, and he did. Our conversation went approximately like this: "There is an answer, if you want it and have what it takes to go for it," I said.

"Of course I want it. What is it?"

"You have to love these competitors of yours."

"What?"

"You have to love them."

"Are you crazy? Did you ever see those fellows?"

"No, I never saw them. But the Bible says you have to love your enemies."

"That is asking too much! It's impossible!"

"I thought you wanted spiritual power."

"I do!"

"I thought we agreed that I was the doctor."

"You are!"

"All right, I prescribe that you love them."

"How do I love them if I hate them?"

"I'll tell you what to do, and it won't be easy. Every day, three times a day, you have to ask the Lord to help those fellows and give them a bigger year in business than you have yourself."

"I refuse to do it!" he shouted.

"Well," I told him, "if you want to have spiritual power, you've got to do it."

I knew one thing about this man: If he made a promise, he would keep it, and he finally assented grudgingly. About ten days later, he came back and told me what had happened. "I went home," he said, "and tried to pray for those so-and-so's and I just could not do it. When I got up the next morning I couldn't do it, and I couldn't do it at noontime. But that night I knew I had to do it or break my promise to you. So I knelt down and said, 'Lord, bless those fellows'—and I named each one—'and give them a bigger business year than You give me.' Then I stopped and looked up and said, 'Lord, don't pay any attention to me, I don't mean a word of it!'"

I could hardly keep from laughing out loud; I knew the Lord must like a fellow like this one.

"But," he went on, "I finally said, 'Okay, Lord, I don't mean it, but I wish you would make me mean it.' So I struggled on all week like that, and finally last night a wonderful thing happened. While I was praying, all of a sudden it seemed as if a great hand came down and took away from my mind this heavy weight that has been there, and I want to tell you that today I am bursting with happiness!"

Of course he was! He did what the Lord told us all to do, and the result was real and wonderful happiness!

Help People to Like Themselves

That man finally made friends with himself. And when that happened, he could love his neighbor. So that is the first step in making friends and keeping them—get yourself straightened out. And what is the second step? It is helping your neighbor think more highly of himself. If you can just do that, you will never have to look around for friends. They will come to you. They will flock to you. You will need a stick to keep them away!

Lord Chesterfield, that wise Englishman, knew this. In his famous letters to his son he said something like this: "My son, here is the way to get people to like you. Make every person like himself a little better and I promise that he or she will like you very much."

That is profoundly true. Do you remember that earlier in the book I told about the professor at college who reprimanded me so severely and told me to improve my performance? Why do I remember him after all these years and love him still, although I was angry at the time? Because he saw a better "me" inside me, and proceeded to drag it out. He made me perform better, and when I did, I liked myself better, and I came to love the man who was responsible, even though it was a rough process. Emerson put it well in one of his memorable sentences: "Our chief want in life is someone who shall make us do what we can." That is indeed the function of a friend.

Do you lack friends? Take an acquaintance, or several acquaintances, study them a bit, then select their best attribute and praise them for it. This doesn't mean fulsome or insincere flattery. It means a fair and friendly recognition of something worthwhile in them. That recognition will increase their self-esteem. And they will eagerly give their friendship to the person who does that for them.

Everywhere you go you will find people who are not living up to the best in themselves. People love to have this best element recognized and coaxed out of them. Sometimes, to be sure, they resist. It is a paradox: they want the best drawn out of them and yet they don't. I see this quite often when I'm preaching (and what is preaching but an effort to draw the best out of people?). Some members of the congregation come to church because they know they need to be improved, and yet they hold back as if saying, "Well, get it out of me if you can!" Finally, if their lives are improved, it isn't the minister who does it. It is Jesus Christ, whose servant the minister tries to be. And that is one of the many reasons people love Jesus. He brings the best out of them and is therefore their best friend.

Another simple but basic way to make friends is to help people, not just when they ask for help but also when you see that they need it. I remember reading a newspaper story about a filling-station operator named Sam. With winter coming on, somebody sold Sam a snowplow, the kind you attach to the front of a car. When the first heavy snow came, he used it to clear the snow away from his gas pumps. It took only a few minutes. He looked across the street and saw a man's driveway all snowed in. The man was vainly trying to get his car out. Sam went over and cleaned his driveway. Then he went on to the next house. Soon he had cleaned out the driveways of twenty-nine houses.

Now where do you think all those people went the next time they needed gas? They went to see their friend Sam, of course. Later on, the story said, the Small Businessmen's Association had a meeting in Washington to study methods and techniques of successful salesmanship. They had heard about Sam, for by this time he was cleaning the driveways of several hundred homes each winter. Not only that, but anyone in the community who had a problem or wanted an errand done would call on Sam because he would take on anything from baby-sitting to delivering groceries to shut-ins. The Small Businessmen's Association heard that Sam was selling more gasoline than anyone in his area, so they asked him to come and give his magic formula. Sam, to their astonishment, simply told them he got his formula out of the Bible, where it says, "Love one another" (John 15:17).

Indeed, that is the most practical, sensible, hardheaded

advice in this world! Businessmen used to come around and complain to me about Christianity's being theoretical. It is theoretical, all right. It is the soundest kind of theory, because it works. I promise you that any business run by people who love their employees and love the people they serve, and who treat them all with loving-kindness, will have black figures, not red ones, in its ledgers. It is a law as inexorable as the law of gravity.

So there are really four steps you must take if you want to make friends and keep them. First, you must examine yourself and get rid of the characteristics that alienate other people. Second, you must make a conscious and deliberate effort to help other people find greater self-esteem. Third, you must go to their aid and assist them over the rough spots in the road of life. Fourth—and most important of all—you must love them, genuinely love them.

People Love You When You Love Them

Human beings always know when you love them—and they respond with love. That is the ultimate basis of friendship. That is what binds people together and holds them together. One of our most beloved entertainers, Will Rogers, used to say he never met a man he didn't like, which guaranteed him endless friends, because no one could be found who didn't like Will Rogers.

I once knew a quiet and likable man named Charlie who ran a grocery store in Pawling, New York, the small town where Ruth and I own an old 1830 farmhouse. Pawling has a population of maybe four thousand people. Charlie ran a chain grocery store for about twenty years, and then the company withdrew from the town. Charlie spoke to me and asked, "Do you think I could run a store of my own? I don't have much capital, but the company said I could have the equipment, and they would give me an inventory to start with."

"Sure you can," I said. I knew that Charlie loved people, and that people loved him. So he took the store, and the day after it opened I went in, and Charlie and I went into one of the back rooms and sat there among the cracker barrels and cartons, and Charlie said, "I want to dedicate this store to God." So he and I had a prayer of dedication.

Later, I used to watch him wait on people. One afternoon a woman came in looking tired and worn. Charlie said to her, "Mary, I'm glad you bought some of that cheese. That is a great New York State cheese, and I know what a good cook you are. Your husband and children are going to have a wonderful supper tonight. Macaroni and cheese cooked by loving hands ... you can't beat that!" The woman stood up straighter and a wonderful smile came over her face. She picked up her groceries and went out, strengthened by the knowledge that the man who had sold them to her was interested in her as a person.

A year or two later one of those big, modern supermarkets opened up only a short distance from Charlie's little store. He asked me, "Do you think I can survive the competition from this big, new supermarket?"

I said, "Just go on loving people, Charlie. You'll be all right."

Well, he was. And when Charlie finally died, his was one of the biggest funerals Pawling ever saw. It seemed as though the whole town turned out to pay tribute to a quiet grocer who loved his fellow human beings.

Never forget it: The way to friendship and the way to happiness is through the wisdom of the wisest Man who ever lived, the Man who said, "A new commandment I give unto you, That ye love one another..." (John 13:34).

Follow that principle and you will find fulfillment for one of the deepest needs of human nature, the desire to be esteemed, and liked, and loved.

16
The Most Important Image of All

Throughout this book, I've talked about the value of imaging in many of the key areas of living. But there is one image that is more important than all the other images combined: the image that you have of yourself.

"As a man thinketh in his heart," the Bible says, "so is he" (*see* Proverbs 23:7). In other words, as you see yourself, so you are.

If you firmly image that you are a person destined for success, success is what you ultimately will have. If you are convinced that you will fail, failure will stalk you no matter where you go. If you think scarcity, it will befall you. If you image abundance flowing to you, it will flow.

The universe is like a great echo chamber: sooner or later what you send out comes back. If you love people, that love will be reflected back to you. If you sow anger and hatred, anger and hatred are what you will reap. If you think mainly of yourself and your own interests, people will never be drawn to you. If you put others first and yourself last, everyone will be your friend.

If you have a mental picture of yourself as an inferior

person, you *will* be inferior, because you will act in a timid and ineffective manner. If you go to a meeting convinced that all others present are brainier or better informed than you are, you will sit there and never open your mouth, although quite possibly you have good ideas and worthwhile contributions to make. You will be tongue-tied by your own low opinion of yourself.

On our last trip to Hong Kong, Ruth had an appointment with a dressmaker, which left me with some time on my hands. Walking through the narrow side streets of fascinating Kowloon, I came upon a tattoo parlor run by an elderly Chinese practitioner of this ancient and venerable art. In the window of his shop were displayed the various decorations that could be imprinted on your skin if that sort of embellishment appealed to you: flags and patriotic slogans, anchors and daggers, skulls and crossbones, mermaids, and so on. But the one that caught my eye was a somber phrase: *Born to lose.*

This interested me so much that I went into the shop and asked the proprietor if he spoke English, which he did to some extent. Then I asked him about the *Born to lose* tattoo. Did people really ask to have that permanently imprinted on themselves?

Yes, he said, occasionally they did. The last customer who wanted it had had it emblazoned on his chest.

"Why on earth," I asked him, "would anyone want to be branded with a gloomy slogan like that?"

The old Chinese man gave an oriental shrug. "Before tattoo on chest," he said, "tattoo on mind!"

How true, I thought, *and how sad*. The born loser was not *born* that way at all. But if he permitted a sense of inferiority to take possession of his mind, if he allowed his self-image to become tinctured with the dye of inadequacy and failure, then a loser is what inevitably he would be.

How does a person gain and keep a strong, serene, confident concept of himself or herself? That is a big question, and there is a twofold answer. You do certain things that enhance and strengthen that image, and you avoid certain things that damage it. Let us take a look at the latter first.

There are three deadly emotions that rob a person of the

normal degree of self-esteem that is so important. Those grim, unwelcome visitors are fear, guilt, and doubt. If any one of them becomes dominant in your life, your self-image is going to suffer. Let us take a look at each one and see what can be done to neutralize their baleful power.

There is an old Russian proverb that says, "A hammer shatters glass but forges steel." The hammers of life are bound to hit each of us, sooner or later. And one of these hammers is that ancient problem of the human spirit known as fear.

From the time when they are little children afraid of the dark, people have to wrestle with this adversary, and the battle continues all through life. Sometimes fear is so great that it shatters people. They lose their confidence, they withdraw from life, their image of themselves shrinks to the point where they no longer believe they can cope with hardship, or illness, or economic problems, or whatever is threatening them. And once their belief in their own competence is lost, it is hard to get it back.

But other people facing the same kind of difficulties react differently, because they have faith. When the hammer of fear hits them, they don't shatter. On the contrary, they are forged into stronger human beings. Through such forging it is possible to become a person who can stand firm, look any fear in the eye, and say, "In the name of God, I am no longer afraid."

What a glorious status to attain! And how is it done? How do you maintain a self-image that enables you to handle fear? The secret lies in a single word: *trust*. Suppose you come to a point where you no longer believe you have what it takes to deal with a situation. Your self-image is weakened. You are afraid you may lose your conviction of competence. What do you do? Well, you relinquish the frightening situation to God. You put it in His hands. You leave it with Him. And you trust him absolutely, because you remember that He said, "Fear thou not; for I am with thee: be not dismayed; for I am thy God: I will strengthen thee; yea, I will help thee..." (Isaiah 41:10). That is the solemn promise of Almighty God. He made it so that we fearful human beings would believe it, and accept it, and be strengthened by it.

Complete trust—it is the most protective and sustaining emotion that the human mind can feel. We experience it as small children when a nightmare terrifies us or a thunderstorm crashes around us in the dead of night. What do we do? We get up, panic-stricken, and scurry to our parents' room, where mother or father lets us into bed, comforts us with encircling arms and soothing words, and finally takes us back to our room, calmed and reassured and ready to go on with the business of living. They don't turn away and they don't make fun of our fears. They offer love and support until the danger and the terror are past.

And God, the Father of us all, is like that. A simple analogy, yes, but that is the essence of most profound ideas: they are simple.

Sometimes complete trust produces results that are beyond the grasp of human understanding. Not long ago I was reading a collection of stories written by members of our armed forces—army, navy, and air force veterans telling of extraordinary experiences they had had.

Adrift in the Pacific

One of the stories was by a navy machinist's mate named Pete Mesaro. Pete was on a PT boat far out in the Pacific Ocean. The sea was rough. Somehow, in the early hours of the morning, while it was still dark, he was hurled against a stanchion, felt great pain in his leg, and toppled into the ocean. No one saw him go overboard. When he came to the surface, the PT boat was racing away from him. He was alone in a vast expanse of sea.

Finally the first faint streaks of dawn lighted up the sky and slanted across the waters. His leg pained him; it was bleeding. Then, to his horror, he saw the black triangular fin of a shark break the surface not thirty feet away. It was making a slow circle around him. His body went so tense with fright that he could hardly breathe. He knew that the blood escaping from his leg had attracted the shark—and would attract others.

Pete was a sincere Christian boy. He prayed—not to be saved, because he didn't think that was possible. He just prayed to God to make the end come quickly and then take his soul to heaven.

"But as I prayed," he wrote, "a strange thing happened." His mind went back across the years to the classroom in the Sunday school he had attended as a child. There was a life-size cardboard cut out figure of Jesus in the corner of that room, and under it in large print were the words BEHOLD, I COME QUICKLY: BLESSED IS HE THAT BELIEVETH (*see* Revelation 22:7). But now he realized that the figure wasn't cardboard at all. It was Jesus Himself, actually speaking those words and coming toward him across the waters with outstretched arms. Indescribably elated, Pete began to swim toward Jesus.

Incredibly, the shark seemed to retreat as Pete swam forward. Then a second shark appeared, and both came at him from converging angles. But the hope that the image of Jesus had given him was stronger than his fear of the sharks. He lashed out at them, splashing and kicking like a madman.

Then the unbelievable thing happened. An American destroyer had come over the horizon. A lookout saw the frantic splashing and realized something was amiss. At flank speed the destroyer came up and lowered a boat with riflemen who drove the sharks away. Pete barely remembered strong arms lifting him into the boat. But before passing out from shock and exhaustion, he saw again the figure of Jesus with arms outstretched.

A miracle? What is a miracle? It is a wonderful occurrence beyond the reach of our analytical understanding. I believe that in this instance, a man completely lost himself in an ecstatic realization of the love and protective presence of God. Had he died, he would have died at peace. But now he lives at peace, knowing that there is nothing in life to be afraid of, so long as we trust God.

Trust really does drive out fear. The other night Ruth and I were coming back to New York from Albuquerque via Dallas. The Texas weather was good, but as we flew on toward New York it became worse and worse. Impenetrable cloud vapor enveloped our plane. It rocked and shuddered from violent wind gusts. We were told to prepare for landing at La Guardia, and we buckled our seat belts, but we could see nothing. Suddenly the swirling mist parted for a moment, and I saw below us the lights of one of New York's great bridges. The tall towers looked close enough to touch. Then suddenly the plane zoomed upward. The pilot had been told by the control tower to go around and make another approach. The cabin was very quiet. Nobody said anything, but you could feel the strain in the air. The faces of the flight attendants were tense.

Now, I am no hero in the sky. But this time, in a situation that certainly was nerve-racking, to say the least, strangely enough neither Ruth nor I felt any fear. We prayed silently for the pilot, asking that he be given calmness and good judgment. We prayed for the men on the ground who were guiding us by the invisible beacon of radar. I remember thinking that it was amazing how many unseen people we trusted—the designer of the airplane, the maintenance crews that serviced the great engines, the hydraulic systems, the communications networks, the weather forecasters . . . we trusted our lives to all of them, almost without thinking.

The pilot made another approach. Again he pulled up sharply. This time he told us, in a calm, almost laconic fashion, that at the last moment he had spotted another aircraft on the runway where we had been cleared to land. Tension in the cabin mounted even higher, but still Ruth and I were not afraid. We felt that we were in the hands of the Lord, and that those strong, loving, capable hands would put us down in a safe landing on the third attempt. I believed that. I trusted that it would happen. I imaged it happening. And so neither of us felt fear.

On the third attempt, the captain set his big bird down with a barely perceptible jolt. The whole cabin burst into heartfelt applause! Later I met the husband of one of the flight attendants and he told me that his wife said those first two attempts at landing were the most hazardous and terrifying moments of all her ten years in the air.

Perhaps, as we grow older, we begin to lose our fear of dying, which is certainly one of the most basic and universal of all fears. It is a fear that to some extent is kept alive by the paganism of the world, which regards death as the end of everything. Certainly I am in no hurry to leave this world. I enjoy life enormously. I'm having a wonderful time. It is a lovely world, and very few of us want to exchange it for death, which so often has been associated in our minds with gloom and sadness.

But trust can overcome even this most elemental of all fears. Can you believe that a God who has given us this beautiful world would, when we die, put us in a place of ugliness? Can you believe that the God who gives us such precious experiences here on earth would suddenly extinguish us like a candle flame? Do you believe that a God whose every manifestation here is of life and vitality and creativity will suddenly change and consign us all to death and destruction? I have never seen any sign that God is so capricious. The very orderliness of the universe belies it. The seasons follow one another in absolute regularity. The stars come out in the skies nightly in the same old wonderful patterns. Even those heavenly bodies that come only periodically return on the stroke of the minute. When I was a child I saw Halley's comet. It had been predicted many years before that it would come back at that precise time, and it did. And in a few years now it will come again. On time. To the split second.

Can you believe that a God of such exquisite order will suddenly become a God of disorder, that He will be kind to you at one time and cruel to you at another? There is no logic in such thinking. Faith rejects it, also. Faith as well as reasoning says a great *No* to any such proposition. The mystical expereinces of life deny it. The longer I live, the more I think about death, the more convinced I am that when we finally come to it, death will be just another expression of God's unbounded love and beauty.

So don't let any kind of fear warp and shrink the image you have of yourself. "Lo, I am with you alway," said Jesus, "even unto the end of the world" (Matthew 28:20). With an assurance like that, we need never be afraid.

Damaging Effect of Guilt

The second image-damaging emotion, not as common as fear but still common enough, is guilt. How can you possibly think well of yourself if your own conscience condemns you? You can't. Even when you try to stifle the voice of conscience (and many people try to persuade themselves that they can do just that), the sense of wrongdoing will take its toll one way or another. Sometimes in the form of a physical affliction. Sometimes in a change in mental faculties. Sometimes in a deep, unacknowledged sickness of the soul: loss of vitality, of enthusiasm, of self-confidence. You can't avoid it any more than you can avoid the law of gravity.

People were more aware of this a generation ago than they are now. The church saw to that. When I was a youngster growing up in the heartland of America, there was a lot of talk from the pulpit about sin. Preachers didn't pussyfoot around. They didn't invent fancy theological terms for wrongdoing that watered it down to a comfortable level. They called sin by its rightful name, and when they banged on the Bible and said that the wages of sin is death, everybody knew what they were talking about. Adultery. Fornication. Drunkenness. Dishonesty. Deceitfulness. Selfishness. Greediness. Lust. Laziness. The list was long and it was specific. If you gave in to any of these things, you were a sinner, and the word came down, tough and uncompromising, that you had better straighten up and do better or else you were in danger of losing your immortal soul. You would go straight to hell, was the blunt way it was told.

Through the years, I have seen many physical manifestations of a hidden sense of guilt. I remember one woman who suffered from a terrible rash and itch every time she attended a church service. Why? Because these were merely external manifestations of a deep spiritual malady inside of her, mainly guilt for certain transgressions that she was trying to repress and hide. Coming to church triggered and heightened that sense of guilt. Only by confession and repentance was she able to cure the internal problem. When she did, the rash disappeared.

I remember another case years ago in Syracuse. One of my close friends, an ear, nose, and throat specialist, told me of a woman who suffered greatly from a sinus condition that no medical treatment seemed to alleviate. The doctor was astute enough to suspect that some spiritual dislocation lay behind this physical problem, and he asked me if I would help with the case. After several conversations, it became evident that the woman hated her mother, who was long since deceased. In a way, she had a valid reason for hating her mother. When another child in the family—her mother's favorite—died, the mother screamed at this daugther, "Oh, why wasn't it you? I wish it had been you!" A dreadful, hurtful thing. But the guilt the woman felt for hating her mother was so strong that it showed up as an infection in her sinuses! Once we persuaded her to forgive her mother, to understand that the grief-racked woman was not entirely responsible for what she had said, the chronic sinus condition began to subside.

If you are a creative person, your self-image is of crucial importance. If you are a writer, you must believe that your thoughts and ideas are worthy of respect and attention. But if you lose your respect for yourself, you begin asking yourself why anyone else should pay attention to you. You begin to think your work is not worthy of being read. The result can be paralysis of the creative faculty.

A few years ago, a very well-known writer who was an acquantance of mine called me up. "Norman," he said, and his voice was hoarse with tension, "I have to see you. I'm in great trouble."

I asked him what he meant by that, but he wouldn't give me an explanation. He just kept saying that he had to see me right away. He lived in a nearby town, so I finally told him to come on over to our farmhouse in Pawling.

When he arrived, I was shocked at the change in the man. He was haggard and grim. He looked sick—and indeed he was sick, with a soul sickness that went very deep. He told me that he could no longer write. This had produced financial problems so acute that he could no longer sleep. I had the feeling that he was carrying an enormous load of guilt, that he had been carrying it for years, and that it had finally caught up with him. "You'd better get it off your chest," I told him. "For the moment, at least, I'm your pastor. So come clean [I used that phrase deliberately] with me. But," I warned him, "you can't hold anything back, or you will be wasting your time and mine. You will have to get it all out, whatever it is."

I took him out to a little room over our barn, where we wouldn't be disturbed. And he began to talk. He poured out a torrent of poisonous memories, mostly of sexual misconduct, that went back for years. It was a grim recital. I wondered how his image of himself as a writer had survived as long as it had. Now that image was shattered, and it would require exorcising to rebuild it.

So we began the process, using the old, time-tested techniques of confession and repentance, followed by the promise of forgiveness. I made him kneel on the rough floorboards of the old barn, and I knelt with him while he poured out, before Almighty God, his guilt and misery and his desire to change. I told him that God was faithful to forgive sins where there was true repentance and that, as God's representative, I could assure him that he had that forgiveness. It was a moving and exhausting experience for both of us, but there was a new light on his face, and I knew that he would make a new start and eventually recover his lost creativity.

And so he did. But how much pain could have been avoided if he had just had the good sense to know that moral laws cannot be broken with impunity—not if you want the self-image that determines your course in life to remain strong and confident.

The third great stumbling block to a serene and confident self-image is doubt. Doctor Charles Mayo, of the famous Mayo Clinic, said, "I have never known a man to die from overwork, but I have known many to die of doubt."

Doubt is the enemy of faith. People who have developed real faith have a strong hold on an actual life-force. Faith channels into you the mysterious power that recreates and reproduces health, vitality, and energy.

But doubt can block this flow of power. A skeptic puts himself outside the magic circle. If you repudiate the reality and power of God, you are really repudiating everything, including your own importance and the reason for your own existence.

The value of achieving the absence of doubt and going on to success is illustrated by the brilliant career of a famous big-league baseball pitcher. Following is a story about him from the Baltimore *Sun*:

> In the aftermath of the best season of his career, one in which he won 25 games for the Baltimore Orioles and a Cy Young Award for himself, Steve Stone was asked: "How do you explain going from an 11–7 record in 1979 to a 25–7 record in 1980?"
>
> "I knew I had to realign my thinking about pitching," said Stone. "I knew I had to become a positive thinker in the highest form. I had heard about positive thinking, and that most people only paid it lip service. But what did it really mean? It was not enough just to win tonight. I had to take a philosophy and put it into a system I could work with, something that would hold for the rest of the season and the future. It's an easy thing to bring out; it all depends on the price you're willing to pay."
>
> The input to this new philosophy were "creative visualization, positive thinking and meditation." And to this day, Stone can't offer a better practical explanation, than, "I just seemed to concentrate more on the mound. Instead of hoping I can get somebody out, I know I can get him out.
>
> "It starts with almost bragging to yourself," he said. "You tell yourself things, almost to the point you laugh at yourself and say, 'Yeah, sure.' But then you have to erase all the negatives you have dealt with over the years and start replacing them with positives. It's almost like a brainwashing situation. You have to relearn the task, and relearn how to deal with it physically, psychologically and emotionally. I have reached the point now that I know I'm a winning pitcher, and I'll be a winning pitcher as long as I'm in the game."

If you are a doubter, you cannot really answer the basic questions of life: Why am I? Where did I come from? Where am I going? What am I doing here? And, naturally, if you are a skeptic, your unconscious mind gets a little confused and discouraged. "If this person doesn't know what he is doing here," it says to itself, "why should I bother to help him move in this direction or that? It makes no difference anyway, so I don't think I'll bother."

So, lack of faith can set up a profound existential uneasiness. An exceptionally strong personality may struggle on regardless, but it takes tremendous effort, and if such a person does achieve any significant success it is in spite of himself, because his self-image has no solid, unshakable base.

Even when faith is present, many people suffer from acute self-doubt. Sometimes I think such people should pray at least once a day the prayer attributed to some old Scotsman: "Oh, Lord, give me a higher opinion of myself." I don't mean we should be arrogant or conceited. I mean we should be aware of the enormous potential the good Lord has put into each of us, and move forward with the kind of assurance and confidence that He wants us to have. Sometimes when I sense a kind of gloom or despondency in people, I feel like shouting at them, "Wake up! Cheer up! You are greater than you think! Get rid of self-doubt! Replace it with faith—faith in God, faith in yourself, faith in the future. And nothing shall be impossible for you!"

When your self-image is weakened by doubt, you have a strong tendency to exaggerate the size of the difficulties facing you. Have you heard the story about the little boy who was plagued at school by an overgrown bully who lived on the same street he did? One day this boy was sitting on his front porch with a new telescope his father had bought him, but he was looking into the large end of it.

"Bill" his father said, "that is not the way to use a telescope. Use the other end. That makes the object you are focused on look bigger."

"But I'm looking at Harry," the boy explained, "and I don't want him to look bigger. This way I'm making him look small, and I'm not afraid of him."

The best way to look at difficulties is with hope and confidence. How sad it is to hear people going around saying, "Oh, my! How sick I am! How old I'm getting! How much trouble I have!" If they would just adjust their spiritual telescopes by getting their minds filled with faith and the love of God, they would be saying, "I have been sick, but I'm getting better fast! I'm not old; why, I feel better than I did ten years ago! There are a lot of troubles facing me, sure, but I have the wisdom and strength to overcome them!"

Do you recall the story of the little locomotive that we all had read to us when we were children? I think it was called *The Little Engine That Could*, and it is quite a profound parable, as children's stories often are. The little engine was called upon to pull a heavy train of cars over a steep hill. His brothers and sisters all decided the effort was too much for them; they gave up or refused to try. But the little engine had a different image of himself. He hitched himself to the train and began to pull. "I think I can, I think I can, I think I can," he puffed, slower and slower, as he labored up the hill. And when he reached the crest and started down the other side, he huffed triumphantly, faster and faster, "I thought I could, I thought I could, I thought I could!" He imaged himself as an overcomer of obstacles— and so he was!

Eight Ways to a Better Self-Image

Well, suppose your self-image is not all it should be. Can you do something about it? Of course you can! A weak self-image is not a natural state of mind. You weren't born with it. A newborn baby has a perfectly sound opinion of himself. No, you acquired it as you went along. You acquired it the way you acquire any other characteristic, good or bad: You *practiced* it. You practiced it into your mind, and what you practice *in* you can practice *out*. So here are eight suggestions designed to help you do just that.

1. *See yourself always as a child of God*. This is the greatest of all antidotes to fear. "If God be for us, who can

be against us?" said Saint Paul (Romans 8:31). It is a question that calls for no reply, because the answer is obvious.

Of course, to see yourself as a child of God requires faith that God exists, that He did create you, and that He cares about you. And how do you get such faith? You make up your mind that you want it, you need it, and you are going to have it. Then you go after it.

You can take faith in, like medicine, in various ways. Through the eye, for instance. You can read the Bible and let its great message of faith and healing drive out the doubt thoughts and the fear thoughts. Or through the ear. You can go to church and listen to the stirring hymns and anthems. You can hear the reading of the Scripture. You can listen to a sermon. You can also take in faith simply by observing the miracles of creation that surround you. The starry heavens, the vast and restless ocean, the mighty mountains, the flowers in springtime—can anyone believe they all happened by accident or by chance? "Be still," the Bible says, "and know that I am God" (Psalms 46:10). In your quiet moments, see yourself as His creation, as His child, and your self-image will have a foundation that will never be shaken.

2. *Stand in front of the mirror and take a good look at yourself.* First check your external appearance. Do you look discouraged or defeated? Make yourself stand straight and tall. Put a smile where that frown was. If your clothes seem drab or forlorn, do something about them. Your appearance reflects and affects your image of yourself; if you improve one, you will begin to improve the other.

Then look at the inner person. Do you lack energy and confidence? Are you convinced that your major goals are beyond your reach? Do you doubt your basic ability to cope with life? If you have such qualms or uncertainties, admit that you have them—but also tell yourself that with God's help, you are going to do something about them. Say a quick prayer, asking that a normal degree of self-esteem and self-confidence may be yours. Remind yourself that a weak self-image can be changed into a strong self-image at any stage of life. It is never too late—and the time to begin is now. Image yourself with an improved self-image! Believe that you will get results, and you will.

3. *Decide to treble your capacity for imaging.* If you consistently picture the best—not the worst—happening to you, powerful forces will work to bring about the thing you are visualizing. This is the central theme and message of this book, and it is true, but you will never know it is true until you have experimented with it yourself. Agnes Sanford, the famous healer, wrote in her book *The Healing Light*, "One way to understand a hitherto unexplored force of nature is to experiment with that force intelligently and with an open mind." Exactly so.

Never doubt it. What is imaged in your mind tends to actualize itself in fact. The pyramids of Egypt, the Parthenon, Saint Peter's in Rome, the great soaring bridges of New York, all exist in fact. But once they existed only as an idea in somebody's mind—and that is when their real existence began. Somebody imaged them—and eventually those images took on form and substance. That is the sequence: first the germ of the idea, then the image of the idea, then the energy and determination to clothe it with reality, and finally the triumphant reality. Put that sequence to work for you, and your self-image will expand and grow.

4. *Practice what you do well, and then learn from your successes.* Nothing builds confidence—and with it a strong self-image—like the repetition of superior performance. All good athletes know this: a crack golfer doesn't choose to remember or dwell on the unsuccessful shot. He holds in his mind the image of the spectacular shots he has made in the past, knowing that that memory will help him repeat them in the future.

If you have a skill—and everyone has something they do well—seize every opportunity to exercise that skill. If you bake good cookies, bake them every chance you get. If you don't need them, give them away: the thanks and praise you get will strengthen your self-image. After a somewhat shaky start many years ago, I have become a reasonably proficient public speaker. Now I draw strength and reassurance from reaching an audience, feeling people respond. It reinforces my image of myself as a person whose purpose is to help people over the rough spots in life.

So practice what you do well—and draw strength and confidence from your successes.

5. *Condition your unconscious mind with spiritual power principles*. The best way to do this is to memorize key Bible passages and repeat them over and over until they sink down into your unconscious mind and become part of it. If your unconscious mind accepts these principles, tremendous energies can be released—energies that may change your life and your self-image completely.

At a Rotary Club luncheon in Hong Kong a year or two ago, I heard a Chinese businessman give a remarkable talk. He had come to Hong Kong as a penniless refugee from Red China, with a wife and eight children. They had no money, no possessions, no friends; just the ragged clothes on their backs.

But these people were strongly believing Christians. The man had in his pocket a frayed copy of the New Testament. And in that little book was a line of Scripture that he had committed to memory, a line written nineteen hundred years ago by Saint Paul: "I can do all things through Christ which strengtheneth me" (Philippians 4:13).

That Chinese refugee believed those words because he had imprinted them on his conscious mind. And his unconscious mind had accepted them, too. He believed that with Christ as his ally and guide he could do anything—not just some things, but *all* things. And so he saw himself succeeding in Hong Kong despite all the odds against him. He imaged himself rising out of poverty to modest prosperity and finally to affluence. He even designed a kind of verbal-mathematical formula that he passed along to his hearers at the luncheon. It went like this: I believe plus I can plus I will equals I did.

That triumphant formula, added to that powerful assertion from Saint Paul, erased all doubts from that refugee's mind. And when doubt was banished from his self-image, he was able to move ahead with giant strides.

6. *Sensitize yourself to the beauty and variety and excitement of living*. Don't just take it all for granted. Are

you ever fascinated by the infinite variety of form and color, light and shadow, that surround you? Do you ever walk out at night just to feel the charm and mystery of the stars? Are you thrilled when you see a crescent moon appearing through the branches of a tree or over a shadowy rooftop? Do you get excited about the wonderful discoveries and happenings going on in the world? Do you reach out for new books as they come off the press, searching for the thoughts and wisdom of the leaders of our generation? Do you follow with keen interest the political, international, and sociological movements of today? In other words, are you alive? Surely something is wrong if you are not! Life is so thrilling that it should seem to us like an ever-changing, wonderful play.

And what has this to do with self-image? A great deal. If you feel you are a vital part of the marvelous tapestry of living, aware of it, immersed in it, then you are going to think and act with enthusiasm and confidence and assurance. If you see yourself merely as a bystander, an onlooker, a hesitant observer, rather than a participant, your self-image will reflect that concept.

Life is a marvelous gift. Accept it. See it, hear it, touch it, smell it, taste it . . . live it!

7. *Control your emotions*. If you don't, they may push you into situations that could seriously damage or weaken the image you have of yourself.

They can also damage you physically. Take anger, for example. There is a saying in one of the South Sea Islands— Tahiti, I think—that goes like this: "Man who gets angry quickly, gets old quickly."

If you let your emotions dominate your reason, you may be led into situations that can be devastating to your self-esteem—that is, your self-image. I remember the case of a woman whose husband went out to look for employment on the West Coast. He left her, with their small child, on the East Coast until he was sure he had the right job. Three or four months went by. She was lonely and unhappy, and when an old admirer asked her to go out for dinner she accepted. Emotions took over and she found herself drawn into an affair.

Then, unexpectedly, her husband sent word that he had a good job and wanted her to come to him and bring their child so that the family could be reunited. Suddenly she realized she would have to face her husband, and her self-image began to fall apart. She was guilty. She was afraid.

Almost immediately she found herself unable to talk. She lost her voice and could speak only in a faint whisper. It was as if her mind was trying to help her out by making it impossible to confess to anyone what she had done.

The husband was notified that his wife had some kind of throat trouble, and would have to be examined by specialists. The specialists could find nothing wrong, no growth or tumor, only that the young woman's vocal cords were slightly separated so that when she tried to speak almost no sound came through.

The doctors concluded that the trouble was psychological, not physical, and they were right. The prospect of rejoining her husband filled the wife with such guilt and terror that she was literally scared speechless. In the end, when she finally brought herself to confess her sin and seek forgiveness, the vocal cords came together again. It was not easy to restore her self-image as a loving, faithful, upright person. But finally she accomplished it.

So it is wise to watch over your emotions, to guard them and control them. Image yourself as a person always in command of yourself, and thus greatly improve the chances that that is the kind of person you will be.

8. *The last and most important suggestion I have to make is simply this: Stay close to Jesus Christ always.* Commit your life to Him. He was the first to teach the power of imaging. He told His disciples, quite plainly, that what they pictured with faith would come to pass. Now, after more than nineteen centuries, scientists and psychiatrists and psychologists are at last beginning to proclaim what the faithful knew all along: He was right.

Christ does not change; He is the same yesterday and today and forever. And the truth of His teaching doesn't change, either. You can count on it, indeed. You can stake your life on it.

The most wonderful thing that can happen to any of us

is to have that most profound of all experiences—to know Jesus Christ personally. You can hear about Him all your life and never really know Him. You can believe that He lived and respect Him and honor Him as a great historical figure and still only know Him academically.

But when at last you find Him and experience His reality, when for you He comes out of the stained-glass windows and out of history and becomes your personal Savior, then you can walk through all manner of darkness and pain and trouble and be unafraid. With Him by your side, you can have the most sublime of all positive images and achieve a sure victory in this life and the next.

About the Author

Norman Vincent Peale is one of the most widely read inspirational writers of all time. In addition to serving as pastor of New York City's Marble Collegiate Church, he is a prominent lecturer, radio host and editor and co-publisher of "Guideposts" magazine.

Classic inspirational titles with undying popularity.

____**Acres of Diamonds.** Russell H. Conwell $2.25
The famous lecture that urges greater appreciation of God-given resources and opportunities.

____**The Christian's Secret of a Happy Life.** Hannah Whitall Smith $2.50
The *only* unabridged, authorized edition of this phenomenal best-seller.

____**The Greatest Thing in the World.** Henry Drummond $2.25
The message that the Scottish writer and lecturer developed from the 13th chapter of I Corinthians.

____**In His Steps.** Charles Sheldon $2.95
A novel about a community who used as a guide for their actions the question, "What would Jesus do?"

____**The Practice of the Presence of God.** Brother Lawrence $2.50
A three-hundred-year-old classic, this is the intimate account of how one man found God.

____**With Christ in the School of Prayer.** Andrew Murray $2.25
One of the world's devotional classics, which teaches the privilege and power of prayer.

ORDER FROM YOUR BOOKSTORE

If your bookstore does not stock these books, return this Order Form to:

Spire Books, Box 150, Old Tappan, New Jersey 07675
Enclosed is my payment plus $.70 mailing charge on first book ordered, $.30 each additional book.

NAME_____

STREET _____

CITY _____ STATE_____ ZIP_____

$ _____amount enclosed ____ cash ____ check
____ money order (no C.O.D.)

GIVE THE TUBE A REST.

GOD CALLING, edited by A.J. Russell 2.95
If God spoke to you, what would He say? Join Two Listeners in hearing the very words of the Living God.

YOU CAN BECOME THE PERSON YOU WANT TO BE by Robt. H. Schuller 2.95
The "minister to millions" demonstrates the life-changing principles that pave the way to truly successful living.

THE MAKING OF A DISCIPLE by Dr. Keith Phillips 2.50
How to nurture new believers to Christ-like maturity, through biblical discipleship.

TO UNDERSTAND EACH OTHER by Paul Tournier 2.25
Dr. Tournier discusses marital problems caused by communication breakdowns and points the way to rebuilding through love and understanding.

THE CHRISTIAN'S SECRET OF A HAPPY LIFE by Hannah Whitall Smith 2.50
More than two million sold! A timeless inspirational classic that continues to revolutionize the everyday lives of ordinary people.

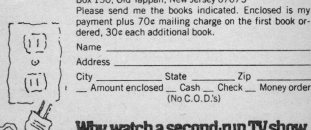

Order from SPIRE BOOKS
Box 150, Old Tappan, New Jersey 07675
Please send me the books indicated. Enclosed is my payment plus 70¢ mailing charge on the first book ordered, 30¢ each additional book.

Name _____

Address _____

City _____ State _____ Zip _____
__ Amount enclosed __ Cash __ Check __ Money order
(No C.O.D.'s)

Why watch a second-run TV show when you can read a first-run book?